The Power-Filled Pastor

The Three God-Given Forces Every Pastor Needs to Succeed in Life and Ministry

A. M. Cartagena

Published by The Finlay & Shadow Company, 230 Country Club Road, Mount Airy, NC 27030

ISBN: 1537148176
ISBN-13: 978-1537148175

DEDICATION

To my darling, Wendy. Your constant love and support is priceless. Thank you for being my *Proverbs 31* wife.

CONTENTS

Acknowledgments   i

1   The Three God-Given Forces   1

2   His Call   7

3   The Communicated   19

4   His Character   32

5   The Need for All Three Forces   46

6   Maintaining the Three Forces   57

7   Avoiding the Force Drain   68

8   Closing Thoughts   76

About the Author   81

Endnotes   82

ACKNOWLEDGMENTS

I am sincerely grateful to every pastor that has provided me with a wonderful model to follow on how to be a power-filled pastor. I am especially grateful to Dr. David Anderson, the Founder and Senior Pastor of Bridgeway Community Church for his support and his leadership. I am also grateful to the elders and leaders at Bridgeway for giving me the space to grow as the Holy Spirit has led me. Finally, I am grateful to Dr. George Miller for being that one friend who always takes my calls and has provided me with great wisdom and leadership.

1 THE THREE GOD-GIVEN FORCES

When I combine my years as a church volunteer, a licensed minister, and an ordained pastor, I have been active in church ministry for over two decades. The lion's share of those years have been spent in a thriving, growing, and effective local church that I believe has served the Lord well in its goals of proclaiming the Gospel of Jesus Christ and of shepherding his disciples. There have surely been some bumps and bruises along the way, but I believe the Lord is pleased with how our church has served His Kingdom. People have come to a saving knowledge of the Lord as a result of our proclaiming and teaching God's Word faithfully; we provide effective care for those going through pain, suffering, and crisis; we have grown steadily in our more than 25 years of ministry and we are known in our community as a generous congregation and a good corporate citizen. While there are many factors we can point to for our success – great leadership from our senior pastor, a clear mission statement that inspires us to action, the hiring of a tremendously talented and faithful team – the greatest reason for our success is our constant commitment to rely on the Holy Spirit and God's Word for the work of our ministry.

Sadly, as my years in ministry have progressed, I have also witnessed some disturbing and devastating situations outside of our church that have left me grieving for many pastors and their respective congregations. I have seen pastors burn out of ministry because they have lacked support from their congregations or have failed to properly delegate any ministry tasks to others in the church. Other pastors have fallen to sin, giving in to the temptation of adultery or financial improprieties. Still there are other pastors who continue to labor in God's vineyard but do so while producing very little fruit – they continuously and consistently open their storefront churches to those same twelve people every week as though they never heard Jesus's call to the Great Commission in *Matthew 28*.

In the last five years dozens of American churches and major ministries have removed their pastors for sin that includes extramarital affairs, emotional abuse of their congregations and staff, financial improprieties involving millions of dollars, and even suspicion of child molestation. I won't name any of the specific pastors, but many of them are well-known names both in the church and among those outside of the church. Interestingly, these pastors belong to various denominations and have different racial-ethnic backgrounds. I state the latter to emphasize the point that temptation and sin are equal opportunity strategies employed by the evil one to derail pastors from their God-given missions.

My personal observations about pastors struggling are supported by research results recently published by the Barna Group. Among the findings in their "The State of Pastors" report: one in three pastors is at risk for burnout; one in five pastors struggles with mental health issues such as depression or addiction; and nearly half of all pastors are in some sort of relational risk.[1] Regarding the last of these findings, the Barna Group report states that pastors often struggle with their family relationships because "the ministry at their current church has been hard on their family."[2] In fact, when pastors were asked whether their current church tenure has proven to be a hardship on their respective families, two out of five pastors answered "somewhat true."[3] Even more alarming, of the one in five pastors reporting a struggle with addiction, "the most common is pornography."[4] Pastors in the United States and in many other countries are feeling beleaguered and under siege – and they are not coping well.

The tragedies that befall many pastors are puzzling, at least in the United States, because of the access we have to so many topnotch seminaries. I have traveled on missions trips to Africa, Latin America, and the Caribbean and one of the universal challenges facing most pastors in these parts of the world is their lack of access to a formal ministry education and the proper discipleship that can be obtained from an excellent seminary. Yet with all of the access we enjoy to this outstanding formal education in the U.S., we still seem to produce pastors who fail to thrive in ministry and even end their respective ministry careers in abject failure.

The mass production of unfruitful and ineffective pastors is also mystifying given that the Bible provides substantial guidance on how to be a power-filled pastor. Specifically, the apostle Paul wrote three letters – known as "the Pastoral Letters" – that are included in the New Testament as *1 Timothy, 2 Timothy*, and *Titus*. Timothy and Titus were Paul's sons in the faith and were young pastors carrying out the work of the ministry under Paul's guidance and instruction. Because he could not be with them personally, he wrote letters directing them on how to be pastors and on how the Church of Jesus Christ should operate in accordance with the Scriptures.

The letters contain practical instructions on subjects such as how to appoint elders and deacons, which widows should be cared for by the church, and how pastors should relate to members of the congregation. There is one specific passage, however, that unlocks three key themes in Paul's letters – themes representing the three God-given forces every pastor actively and simultaneously needs to have a power-filled ministry. The passage is found in *1 Timothy 4:12-16* and it says:

> Don't let anyone despise your youth, but set
> an example for the believers in speech, in

conduct, in love, in faith, and in purity. Until I come, give your attention to public reading [of the Scriptures], exhortation, and teaching. Don't neglect the gift that is in you; it was given to you through prophecy, with the laying on of hands by the council of elders. Practice these things; be committed to them, so that your progress may be evident to all. Pay close attention to your life and your teaching; persevere in these things, for in doing this you will save both yourself and your hearers.[5]

Upon close inspection of this passage, we see three God-given forces that every pastor needs to recognize, and proactively integrate into his life, to experience a power-filled ministry – His Call, The Communicated, and His Character.

In the following chapters, I will present each of these forces as they are defined in the Bible and will subsequently demonstrate how the power-filled pastor really needs all three forces to be working simultaneously in his life for his ministry to bear fruit. Once I present and explain the three forces, I will also explain: (1) what happens when we only have two of the three forces working in our respective lives as pastors; (2) how to best maintain the three forces active; and (3) how to avoid the situations and circumstances that tend to drain pastors as we do ministry and life.

At the end of each chapter, I will provide you with some questions to help you either engage someone in a productive conversation about that chapter's subject or to journal on that chapter for your own personal reflection and meditation. Each chapter will also contain a list of resources related to that chapter's subject in case you desire to engage in deeper study after reading this book.

May the God who calls us to work in His vineyard give

you wisdom and discernment as you read these pages and meditate on the concepts presented herein. I also pray that every pastor and future pastor reading this book will receive the information needed to maximize his individual calling to teach and shepherd those that God brings into his life with passion, excellence, and fruitfulness.

Finally, there are two more groups I pray will read this book – believers in Jesus Christ and church leaders specifically. In writing the Book of Acts, Luke indicated that the Bereans were considered "more noble" because "they received the word with eagerness and they examined the Scriptures daily to see if these things were so."[6] In that same spirit, I pray that this book will help all Christian disciples to interpret the Scriptures so as to discern whether they are being led by a power-filled pastor. My desire is not that you would use the information in this book to attack your pastor, but that you would learn how you might be able to support him to live as a power-filled pastor.

Regarding church leaders, I am praying that this book will be useful as a guide to you in how you select and support the pastors you hire. By church leaders I mean those in the congregation who are tasked with hiring and guiding their respective pastors and providing overall leadership to their specific congregation. This is true whether you are a church congregation led by elders, a board of trustees, or are a congregation-led church. One of the features included in this book are boxes that are scattered through various chapters of this volume titled "To Church Leaders." These boxes contain comments that are specifically directed to church leaders to provide advice and thoughts on various issues of church governance relating specifically to pastors. May the Lord give you wisdom as you exercise authority over your church's pastor and your respective local churches.

Questions

1. What are you hoping to get out of this book?

2. Are you prepared to create a list of action steps to pursue if, after reading this book, you decide that some changes are needed in your life and your ministry?

3. Is there someone you trust – a person of holy character based on God's Word – who can hold you accountable to execute the items on your action steps list?

Recommended Reading

1. John MacArthur. *Pastoral Ministry: How to Shepherd Biblically*. Nashville, TN: Thomas Nelson, Inc., 2005.

2. Charles H. Spurgeon. *Lectures to My Students*. Peabody, MA: Hendrickson Publishers, 2012.

2 HIS CALL

In verse 14 of this book's key passage, the Apostle Paul writes to Timothy, "Don't neglect the gift that is in you; it was given to you through prophecy, with the laying on of hands by the council of elders." This reminder to Timothy – of his need to be both mindful and reliant upon his calling – is an encouragement and teaching that runs all throughout the pastoral letters. In his first letter to Timothy, for example, Paul writes, "Timothy, my son, I am giving you this instruction in keeping with the prophecies previously made about you, so that by recalling them you may fight the good fight, having faith and a good conscience."[7] And in Paul's second letter to Timothy, he explains "Therefore, I remind you to rekindle the gift of God that is in you through the laying on of my hands."[8] The crucial idea behind these and other verses has three implications: (1) Timothy's call to ministry was from God; (2) it is this call that will sustain him as he carries out his ministry duties; and (3) his call involved others who had authority over him.[9]

It's a Call, Not a Job

The call to become a pastor has several important consequences for our respective lives and ministries. The first is the realization that being a pastor is not a matter of obtaining simple employment or the selection of a career. You cannot choose to become a pastor in the same way someone decides to become a police officer, a doctor, or a teacher – you must be called by God to the pastoral ministry. This principle is universally recognized by spiritually mature disciples and anyone who has successfully labored in ministry over an extended period of time. In his book, *The Preacher: His Life and His Work*, John Henry Jowett wrote,

Now I hold with profound conviction that, before a man selects the Christian ministry as his vocation, he must have the assurance that the selection has been imperatively constrained by the eternal God. The call of the Eternal must ring through the rooms of his soul as clearly as the sound of the morning-bell rings through the valleys of Switzerland, calling the peasants to early prayer and praise.[10]

Addressing this issue of calling with his own students, renowned British pastor Charles Spurgeon adds,

In the present dispensation, the priesthood is common to all saints; but to prophesy, or what is analogous thereto, namely, to be moved by the Holy Ghost to give oneself up wholly to the proclamation of the gospel, is, as a matter of fact, the gift and calling of only a comparatively small number; and surely these need to be as sure of the rightfulness of their position as were the prophets; and yet how can they justify their office, except a similar call?[11]

Notice how Spurgeon emphasizes the distinction between the call all Christians receive to build the church and the call to specifically pastor a church. It is the latter call upon which the man of God must stand if he is to succeed in pastoral ministry. A more modern author, Donald Whitney, places the pastor's call in historical perspective by writing:

Famous are the episodes in which God appeared to Moses in the burning bush, called to Samuel in the night, chose David above his brothers, and instructed Elijah to anoint Elisha. These men were divinely appointed, not self-selected. Today, no real pastor becomes a pastor simply by pronouncing himself one – God must call him. By means of what has historically been referred to as the "internal call" of the Holy Spirit, combined with the "external call" of a church that formally recognizes the hand of God upon a man in accordance with the qualifications of 1 Timothy 3, God chooses the pastor.[12]

These comments by Jowett, Spurgeon, and Whitney are clear in supporting the Biblical truth that no man chooses pastoral ministry – he is chosen and is called by God Himself. To attempt to lead a ministry based on your own whims is to invite disaster and to severely damage souls who come to rely on you for spiritual guidance and nourishment.

Not only is this point – that pastors must be called by God – evident in Paul's instruction to his two young pastors, but the idea that pastors are called is supported by the Bible's teaching that Jesus Christ and the Holy Spirit uniquely choose us and anoint us with the gifts required for our specific work in the body of Christ. Regarding Jesus Christ, for instance, we read in *Ephesians 4:11-16*,

And [Jesus] himself gave some to be apostles, some prophets, some evangelists, some *pastors and teachers*, equipping the saints for the work of ministry, to build up the body of Christ, until we all reach unity in the faith and in the knowledge of God's Son, growing into maturity with a

stature measured by Christ's fullness. Then
we will no longer be little children, tossed by
the waves and blown around by every wind
of teaching, by human cunning with
cleverness in the techniques of deceit. But
speaking the truth in love, let us grow in
every way into him who is the head—
Christ. From him the whole body, fitted and
knit together by every supporting ligament,
promotes the growth of the body for building
up itself in love by the proper working of
each individual part. (Emphasis mine)

As we see in this text from Paul's letter to the Ephesians,
pastors are specifically listed as one of the offices of the
church with a specific goal in mind – "to equip the saints
for the work of ministry."[13] More importantly, the office of
pastor is given by Jesus Christ and, therefore, is a calling
from God that brings with it specific gifts and abilities.
Paul, in fact, reminds Timothy of this truth in his second
letter by writing, "Therefore, I remind you to rekindle the
gift of God ..."[14] God, of course, distributes His gifts
through the Holy Spirit, which Paul confirms in writing to
the Corinthians, by explaining,

Now there are different gifts, but the same
Spirit. There are different ministries, but the
same Lord. And there are different activities,
but the same God produces each gift in each
person. A manifestation of the Spirit is given
to each person for the common good ...[15]

The Holy Spirit empowers us, according to our calling in
the church, to carry out the work of the ministry and to do
so for the good of everyone that is part of the church.
Given these passages from *Ephesians* and *1 Corinthians* it
is well within reason to believe that, because the pastor is

called as a distinct office in the church, he will be uniquely gifted by the Holy Spirit to carry out the duties of that specific office.

The Enablement of the Holy Spirit

The latter truth, that God specifically gifts us to carry out our duties as pastors, leads us to the second consequence of the calling to be a pastor – this calling and its concomitant gifting is necessary for us to carry out our duties as pastors. The logical consequence of the Bible's teaching that we are called and uniquely gifted to be pastors must be that those gifts are required for us to carry out our ministry with effectiveness and fruitfulness. We know this to be true from the pastoral letters because Paul writes, "Timothy, my son, I am giving you this instruction in keeping with the prophecies previously made about you, so that *by recalling them* you may fight the good fight …"[16] This is an important point – Paul is specifically telling Timothy that his ability to "fight the good fight" depends on his relying on his call. The 1984 edition of the New International Version translates this verse as follows: "I give you this instruction in keeping with the prophecies made about you *so that by following them* you may fight the good fight."[17] Both of these phrases – "by recalling them" and "so that by following them" – point to the same idea that only pastors called to ministry are equipped to deal with the unique demands of leading and caring for a congregation and that the pastor *must* rely on his calling and his gifts to succeed in ministry.

Once again, this principle that a pastor depends on his call to succeed in ministry, is well known and accepted as true by those experienced in pastoral ministry and church work. In their book, *When Pastors Wonder How*, Sugden and Wiersbe wrote,

The work of the ministry is too demanding
and difficult for a man to enter it without a
sense of divine calling. Men enter and often
leave the ministry usually because they lack
a sense of divine urgency. Nothing less than
a divine call from God could ever give a man
success in the ministry.[18]

To this idea – that our success or failure in ministry
hinges on our calling – Jowett adds, "The assurance of
being sent is the vital part of our commission ... The
absence of the sense of our [calling] will eviscerate a
man's responsibility, and will tend to secularize his
ministry from end to end."[19] The notion that you can
succeed in ministry without being specifically called and
gifted by God is pure folly at best, pretentiousness at
worst; that pretentiousness has been the cause of many
pastors and churches being destroyed and of many souls
falling away from the faith.

In my many years of ministry, I can personally testify
that there are weeks when I only survived because of the
Holy Spirit living in me. In any given week at our church,
I can be walking with a family through the grieving
process as they mourn the loss of their beloved matriarch,
while counseling a married couple contemplating divorce
because they have both had extramarital affairs, while
teaching a class on God's will, and trying to find a way to
pay someone's rent because they lost their job. And in this
same week, my wife may be ill, while one of our children
needs an item for school that hasn't been accounted for in
our family budget, and my father needs me to take care of
a matter for him because he doesn't speak English. I'm
not complaining, but I'm giving you a peek into not only
my life as a pastor, but the lives of many pastors who
have congregations and families to care for and serve. Our
ability to meet all of those needs and to minister well
means relying on the gifts and strength that only the Holy

Spirit can provide and those gifts are only available to us when we are called by the Lord to pastoral ministry.[20]

The Need for Witnesses

I now wish to turn to another of the truths revealed in the pastoral letters – the truth that our calling to be a pastor must be affirmed and confirmed by others. To explain what I mean, I will present a situation that I have seen played out at least twice in our church and that I know has happened at other churches as well. Occasionally, we will get someone who comes to our church and asks if we will allow him or her to teach a class or a Bible study to our congregation. Sometimes they will actually take the bold step of confessing their sincerely-held belief that they have been called to become a pastor.

At our local church, we enjoy encouraging people when they feel called to a specific role in ministry. We will not, however, just immediately place you in the role you request. We take a Biblical approach in that we first give you small assignments and, as you carry those out faithfully, we give you more responsibility according to your gifts, your talents, and your call as the Holy Spirit reveals it through the Scripture.[21] This process has worked well for us in that we have been able to identify and encourage individuals who have been a tremendous blessing to our church through their respective gifts and their individual ministry, many of them as ministers and pastors. This process has also helped us to prevent potentially disastrous situations where we have discerned that someone has been misguided in their belief that they have been called to teach or to become a pastor.

In fact, two specific individuals so strongly believed that they were called to pastor a church that they left our congregation when we would not affirm that "calling" and have started their own churches. Those respective churches have now existed for years and have not experienced any kind of significant growth or have made any substantial impact for the Kingdom and it's no surprise – these well-intentioned individuals have deluded themselves into believing that they have a calling to pastoral ministry that simply isn't there.

NOTE TO CHURCH LEADERS

Church leaders should never be satisfied with hiring a pastor and then sitting back to watch how the church operates. You have an obligation to not just steward the church for your generation, but to set the church up for success for your children and your grandchildren. In that spirit, church leaders should be looking to identify your congregation's future leaders and to confirm the calling God has placed on people in your community as that calling becomes apparent to you. When you come together to pray, you should be asking God to show you who he is calling and ask Him for wisdom on how you can best encourage those who have been called. On a more practical level, you should consider adopting some type of succession plan for the day your current pastor is called to retire or is called home to be with the Lord.

To make my point about the need for a call to be witnessed by others, please allow me to show you that even the Apostle Paul's call to ministry was affirmed and confirmed by others. Paul's call to ministry should be well-known to disciples of Jesus Christ – Paul was on his way to Damascus to arrest and persecute Christians when Jesus himself called him to ministry.[22] There are two specific aspects of his call that are relevant to the idea that calling must be affirmed and confirmed by others.

First, Paul's call was witnessed and affirmed by those who were with him on his Damascus journey. The Bible says in *Acts 9:7*, "The men who were traveling with him stood speechless, hearing [Jesus's voice] but seeing no one." These men were the soldiers accompanying Paul on his quest to arrest Christians and they witnessed his call to ministry. Hence, these soldiers could affirm that Paul was called by Jesus based on what they personally witnessed. And did you know that even Jesus's gifts were obvious to those people who heard him speak so that they could affirm his calling? Matthew records the moment after Jesus preached the Sermon on the Mount by writing, "When Jesus had finished saying these things, the crowds were astonished at his teaching, because he was teaching them like one who had authority, and not like their scribes."[23] Can you really appreciate what this verse is communicating? Joe and Sally Congregant, the people listening to Jesus speak, possessed the ability to discern that his teaching was anointed. When considering a pastoral candidate, therefore, it is both fair and necessary to ask the question, "Is this person surrounded by people who see, and believe in, his call to pastoral ministry?"

Second, after being called by Jesus to ministry, Paul presented himself to church leaders to have his call confirmed.[24] In fact, Paul gives the reason for presenting himself to the church leaders, writing, "I went up according to a revelation and presented to them the gospel I preach among the Gentiles, but privately to those recognized as leaders. I wanted to be sure I was not running, and had not been running, in vain."[25] Did you catch that? Paul wanted to make sure that the church leaders approved of the gospel he was preaching to the Gentiles.

I use Paul as an illustration to support the Biblical truth that a calling to Christian ministry does not happen in isolation nor is self-proclaimed. If Paul needed the church elders to confirm his call, why wouldn't you? A call to ministry must be affirmed by those around us who can be a witness to God's movement in our respective lives and it must be confirmed by church elders who, not only can give witness to God's call, but can guide us in both our doctrine and our walk as pastors.

Because this was true in Paul's life regarding his own calling to ministry, it is a point he made several times in the pastoral letters to his sons in the faith. Timothy and Titus both needed to be reminded of God's call in their individual lives so that they might be encouraged in their ministry work and to remember that, in the end, they are accountable to God for that work. That encouragement and accountability is lived out in the context of the relationship between a pastor and the leaders of the church where he teaches and shepherds.

In fact, for the clergy reading this book I want to share two verses that speak to the higher level of accountability we are held to as pastors. The first comes from *James 3:1*, where Jesus's brother wrote, "Not many should become teachers, my brothers, because you know that we will receive a stricter judgment." And in the Book of Hebrews, the writer instructs the church, "Obey your leaders and submit to them, since they keep watch over your souls as those who will give an account ...".[26] In those quiet moments when I lie in bed and really think about my life as a pastor, these two verses make me shudder in fear. The immensity of the responsibility is great and can only be carried out by the man who has been called and equipped by God Himself to carry out this ministry of the pastorate.

Throughout the remainder of the book, I will be building a model that visually demonstrates the three God-given forces in a pastor's life and how these forces manifest themselves in our respective pastoral ministries. Figure 1 below shows a pastor's call as a simple circle, but throughout the book I will increasingly reveal a model that will demonstrate how each of three forces interact with one another.

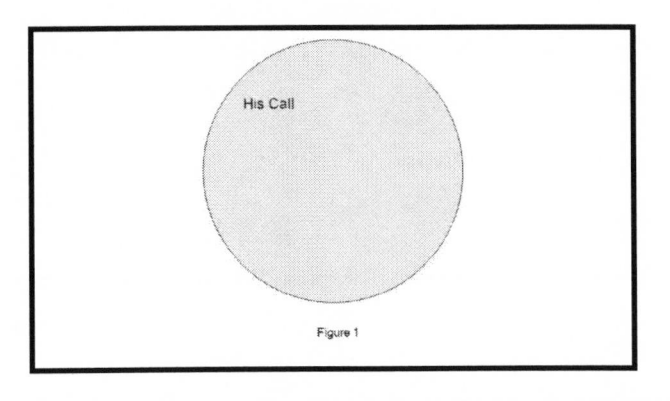

Figure 1

In the next chapter we'll discuss the second God-given force in a pastor's ministry and life – The Communicated. The latter refers to the Holy Scriptures and we will see the foundationally integral part that the Bible should have in an individual pastor's life and ministry.

Questions

1. Can you think of a pastor that you can confidently affirm has a calling on his life? Do you see it in his life and his preaching? Conversely, do you know a so-called pastor that has left you wondering if he possesses sober judgment of self in accordance with *Romans 12:3*?

2. Do you feel God is calling you to pastoral ministry? If so, have you discussed this with your church elders? Do you agree that your call must be affirmed and confirmed by others?

3. Please read *Galatians 2:1-10*. Why did Paul seek out the church leaders? How is this important to pastors? How is this important to you in deciding whether your pastor is power-filled?

Recommended Reading

1. Os Guinness. *The Call: Finding and Fulfilling the Central Purpose of Your Life.* Nashville, TN: Thomas Nelson, 2003.

2. Derek J. Prime and Alistair Begg. *On Being a Pastor.* Chicago, IL: Moody Publishers, 2004.

3 THE COMMUNICATED

In all three of the pastoral letters you will find a phrase that appears nowhere else in Scripture – "sound doctrine." The latter phrase literally means "healthy teaching" and is Paul's way of saying that his young charges should teach the Holy Scriptures so that their respective congregations will know what the Bible says and how to apply the Bible to both their individual lives as well as their lives as a church body. Bobby Jamieson defines "sound doctrine" as, "a summary of the Bible's teaching that is both faithful to the Bible and useful for life."[27]

Paul emphasizes to both of his sons in the faith that being a good and responsible pastor requires: the consistent and reliable teaching of Scripture; that Scripture is the ultimate standard by which all life and conduct is to be weighed; and that our work in the ministry will ultimately be judged, in large part, by how we faithfully teach the Scriptures to our congregations and to those we are discipling for ministry.

The Apostle Paul not only practiced this in his own life and ministry, but he made sure to emphasize it to his young charges. In verse 13 of this book's key passage, Paul writes, "Until I come, give your attention to public reading [of Scripture], exhortation, and teaching." It is a command that he repeatedly makes to both Timothy and Titus throughout the Pastoral Letters. Paul writes to Titus, for example, "But you are to proclaim things consistent with sound teaching."[28] Paul's teaching to his young pastors is of utmost importance to those of us who have been called to shepherd congregations and to make disciples of Jesus Christ. A powerful and Spirit-filled ministry requires a deep and abiding commitment to learning and teaching the Bible as nothing less than the inerrant and inspired Word of God; the Bible is the ultimate guide for how we are to live our lives until Jesus returns for his church. Now if you're currently a pastor reading these words, you might be tempted to think that I am overstating the obvious. Please allow me to share a story that will demonstrate that this point may not be as obvious as you think.

I was practicing law many years ago when I started to sense God's call in my life to pastoral ministry. Once it became clear that God was calling me, my lawyer instincts took over and I prayerfully read as many books and interviewed as many people as I could to determine what this call might mean for my life. There was someone in my extended family that claimed to be a pastor (and was indeed leading a congregation) and so I approached him during a family reunion to ask him how he prepared to preach. My question flowed from my concern that if God was calling me to lead my own congregation, I might not have enough to say every week to people seeking spiritual guidance from me. This "pastor's" response to my question was to say, "Oh, I never study. I just plop my Bible down on the pulpit and whatever page it opens to, I preach from there. I can preach about anything right off the top of my head." He really said this to me. And he said it like he was proud. Not only did I go to sleep that night horrified at the idea that there are people who depend on this man for spiritual guidance and development, but I shuddered to think that there are other so-called "pastors" out there like him.

Years ago, one of the elders of my church affirmed my calling to the pastorate and said this to me – "A call to pastor is a call to study." This elder was simply passing along to me advice that Paul had given to his own sons in the faith. The pastor must study so that he may correctly and powerfully teach God's Word to those under his care. In fact, Paul put it to Timothy like this – "Study to show yourself approved by God, a workman who need not be ashamed, rightly dividing the word of truth."[29] Hence, in this chapter, I want to address the preeminence that the teaching of God's Word must have in a pastor's ministry and to explain why the Bible must be a pastor's highest priority.

The Preeminence of God's Word

In getting you to understand Paul's direction on the importance and priority the teaching of God's Word must have in a pastor's life, I need to take you outside of the pastoral letters for a moment. We're specifically going to the Books of Acts, which records the inception and the growth of the church in the first century.

For many years I have been blessed with the opportunity to teach God's Word to churches and pastors outside of the United States. One issue I see plaguing many churches in these countries is the ignorance, or the unwillingness, of some pastors to delegate many ministry duties to others in their respective congregations. Pastors unwilling to delegate often won't do it because they fear losing their congregations to perceived competitors. Many of these pastors consequently burn out, eventually giving in to temptation or suffering illnesses because they are utterly fatigued. I always take the opportunity to teach these pastors about the need for them to delegate many of their church's routine and mundane tasks and the fact that we are instructed by Scripture to delegate many of these church duties to others.

When I teach these international pastors regarding the need to delegate, I rely on *Acts 6*, where we see an incident involving congregational care. In that Biblical text, the Greek Jews complained to the apostles that their widows were being overlooked in the distribution of food in favor of the Hebraic Jews. Luke explains how the apostles subsequently handled the matter:

The Twelve summoned the whole company of the disciples and said, "It would not be right for us to give up preaching the word of God to wait on tables. Brothers and sisters, select from among you seven men of good reputation, full of the Spirit and wisdom, whom we can appoint to this duty. *But we will devote ourselves to prayer and to the ministry of the word.*"[30]

Did you catch that last verse? The apostles emphasized that their first responsibility to the church was to devote themselves to "prayer and to the ministry of the word." In referring to this same Bible text, Jason Duesing wrote, "While pastors have very diverse day-to-day tasks, in the end they are to focus on praying and preaching."[31] While a pastor must assure that all of the church's duties are carried out, operating a church according to Scripture means being a pastor that knows how and when to delegate important, but often routine, duties to other capable individuals. In this passage of Scripture, we interestingly see how the apostles established the church's first sub-ministry – the Care Ministry – so that they could focus on their foremost priority of teaching God's Word and prayer.

While I have used this passage from the Book of Acts many times to teach the importance of, and the need for, pastors delegating ministry tasks and duties to others in the church, and that the delegation must be to qualified individuals, it is important to understand the reason given for delegating these duties – a congregation's pastor must have, as his first priority, prayer and the teaching of God's Word. This brings us back to Paul's instruction to Timothy and Titus.

Paul's continued emphasis to his sons in the faith – that they must be faithful in teaching the Scriptures as "sound doctrine" – makes complete sense when we look at it through the lens of *Acts 6*. This issue is so important, in fact, that Paul starts his first letter to Timothy by instructing him to challenge false doctrine whenever it is being taught by others. Pastors certainly have responsibility for the care of their congregation as we see, for example, from Paul's instructions regarding the care of widows.[32] But in the end, the pastor's primary responsibility is the preaching and teaching of God's Word.

NOTE TO CHURCH LEADERS

One of the ways church leaders must hold pastors accountable is to make sure they are teaching sound doctrine. I don't advocate leaders choosing *what* a pastor will preach, but that they should focus on *how* the pastor is preaching and teaching. For example, is there a good balance between exegetical and topical preaching? Is the congregation being taught only on Sundays or are they being fed throughout the week? Do the sermons contain a good balance of Scripture and application? In the end, leaders are responsible for checking the fruit – is the congregation growing in holiness and love? A good pastor will always be open to feedback and will rely on it as the Holy Spirit guides him.

The Power of God's Word

Paul, being an excellent teacher, would never simply tell his young pastors what to do. A good teacher always provides the reason or reasons why you are being instructed to specifically do something. And so the question must be asked, why should teaching the word of God be such a high priority for a pastor? The answer lies in *2 Timothy 3:14-17*, where Paul writes to Timothy,

> But as for you, continue in what you have learned and firmly believed. You know those who taught you, and you know that from infancy you have known the sacred Scriptures, which are able to give you wisdom for salvation through faith in Christ Jesus. All Scripture is inspired by God and is profitable for teaching, for rebuking, for correcting, for training in righteousness, so that the man of God may be complete, equipped for every good work.

The short answer to be given regarding priority is that the Holy Scriptures are powerful in what they provide the follower of Jesus Christ and the church for life on earth and beyond. Jamieson puts it this way: "Sound doctrine leads to sound faith, sound hearts, and sound consciences. And these become the fountain from which flows an entire life that is pleasing to God. The aim of sound doctrine is sound living."[33] To better grasp what Paul is teaching here, let's get an understanding of the context of this particular passage.

When Paul urges Timothy to continue in what he has "learned and has firmly believed," he reminds Timothy that he has held these beliefs since youth and then reminds Timothy of the source of those beliefs – his mother Eunice and his grandmother Lois. Earlier in Paul's second letter to his young charge he wrote, "I recall your sincere faith that first lived in your grandmother Lois and in your mother Eunice and now, I am convinced, is in you also."[34] Timothy was a third generation Jew with a Greek father and was obviously trained in his faith by his mother and grandmother.[35] And why is it important to take note of Timothy's training? Because his training included being introduced to the Holy Scriptures.

Now that we understand the context of Timothy's upbringing in the faith, let us now examine why Paul provided this specific guidance regarding the teaching of the Scriptures. The very first point Paul makes about the "sacred writings" is that they "are able to give you wisdom for salvation through faith in Christ Jesus."[36] This is no small point as I write this chapter in September 2017.

There is a very popular and well-known megachurch pastor in the United States that has taught, both through sermons and through the publication of a widely-read book, that first century Christians came to faith in Jesus solely through his resurrection and not through the teaching of the Bible. The apparent foundation for his teaching is that, at least with early first century Christians, the Bible as we currently know it did not exist. The obvious implication of his assertion, whether he intended to make it or not, is that the Bible is not necessary for people to come to salvation. In fact, he even teaches that pastors should avoid using phrases like "The Bible says" or "God's Word says" when preaching or teaching the Bible. This pastor's teaching should be of great concern to other pastors and the church because it denies, by implication, the authority and power of the Holy Scriptures and it is simply inconsistent with the teaching of the Scriptures themselves.

Focus on Paul's very first characterization of the "sacred writings" – that they "are able to give you wisdom for salvation through faith in Christ Jesus." When Paul reminds Timothy that his mother and grandmother introduced him to the "sacred writings," he is referring to, and specifically identifying, what we know today as the Old Testament. Paul's point to Timothy is that even the Old Testament, by itself and because it is the inspired Word of God, is sufficient to point you to Jesus Christ and that your preaching must be based on the Holy Scriptures for you to bring people to a saving knowledge of Jesus Christ. And do you know who agrees with Paul on this point? Jesus Christ himself.

In *Luke 24*, two men are walking to the town of

Emmaus after Jesus had been crucified. Jesus appeared on the road with them, but in a form or method that rendered the two men unable to recognize him. While they shared their despair in losing their Lord and teacher, Jesus's response was to chastise them by saying,

> "How foolish and slow you are to believe all that the prophets have spoken! Wasn't it necessary for the Messiah to suffer these things and enter into his glory?" Then beginning with Moses and all the Prophets, he interpreted for them the things concerning himself in all the Scriptures.[37]

For those readers with no or little theological training, Jesus's reference to "Moses and all the Prophets" is a specific reference to the Old Testament. The truth – that the Old Testament points to Jesus Christ as our Messiah and Savior – is so vital to our faith that when Jesus and these two men joined the other disciples in Emmaus, Jesus felt the need to repeat his lesson to all of the other disciples. We read later, in *Luke 24:44-48*,

> [Jesus] told them, "These are my words that I spoke to you while I was still with you— that everything written about me in the Law of Moses, the Prophets, and the Psalms must be fulfilled." Then he opened their minds to understand the Scriptures. He also said to them, "This is what is written: The Messiah would suffer and rise from the dead the third day, and repentance for forgiveness of sins would be proclaimed in his name to all the nations, beginning at Jerusalem. You are witnesses of these things.

So Jesus not only cites to the Old Testament to

demonstrate that he is the expected Messiah, but he reminds them that he had instructed them accordingly when he was still alive and with them. The very idea that we can bring people to a knowing faith in Jesus Christ separate and apart from the Bible, does not accord with the "sound doctrine" given to Timothy and Titus by Paul. One of Paul's repeated instructions to his sons in the faith is that they preach and teach the Holy Scriptures as their first and highest priority.

The next reason a pastor needs to make the Bible a priority in his ministry is simply because it *is* God's Word. Paul tells Timothy that the Holy Scriptures are "breathed out by God."[38] This phrase in English translates the Greek word *theopnuestos*, which apparently had never appeared in any Greek text (the Bible or otherwise) prior to Paul's writing this letter to Timothy. Ray Van Neste explains that some believe "Paul coined this term from words meaning 'God' and 'breathed,' which is certainly possible. The term stresses the divine origin and thus the authority of Scripture."[39] Paul makes no mention of the human authors here, but specifically characterizes the very words of Scripture as having been "breathed out by God." Hence, in the end, the pastor called by God must teach the Bible as nothing less than the inspired, inerrant Word of God. The pastor must also stress that because the Scriptures are inspired by God and are His very words, they are the ultimate authority for how the disciple of Jesus Christ must live his or her life.

The third reason for making the Bible a priority in our pastoral ministry is Paul's characterization of God's Word as "profitable." Specifically, according to Paul, the Scriptures are profitable for teaching, rebuking, correcting, and training in righteousness.[40] If we break down the Greek words and definitions for each of the key words in this sentence, we would have the following information: "teaching (*didaskalia*) means "doctrine or teaching material;" "rebuking" (*elegchō*) means "to rebuke one so as to lead him to be convicted of his sin;" "correcting" (*epanorthōsis*) means the restoration of one to an upright or right state;" and "training" (*paideia*) means "the whole training and education of children that relates to the cultivation of mind and morals."[41] If we were to summarize what Paul wrote to Timothy in this instance, I believe the message would be this – the Bible as a whole is completely sufficient for teaching and training people to help them transition from a life of sin (by showing them and convicting them of their sin) to a life of being right with God and of being able to live rightly before God. While a pastor can rely on other sources for purposes of illustration and explanation, God's Word is complete in what it offers the world regarding God's character, His wisdom, and His expectations.

Finally, Paul informs Timothy that the use of the Holy Scriptures should result in the man of God being "complete, equipped for every good work." (*2 Timothy 3:17*) In other words, we should ask ourselves whether we are we using the Bible to produce mature Christians that are leading lives of service for the church and the Kingdom of God. As pastors, we should be asking specific and important questions about our ministry. First, are we making disciples in accordance with *Matthew 28:16-20*? Second, is my teaching of the Bible producing a congregation that is equipped for and performing good works or am I creating a community of by-stander Christians? Third, have I created spectator Christians who solely come to see a show every week? Finally, if I were to ask the people I shepherd whether they feel prepared to evangelize and care for God's people, would they say "yes?"

There is one more issue that needs to be addressed with regards to teaching sound doctrine. The issue goes to a pastor's decision in whether to teach the Bible exegetically or topically. There are some pastors and bible scholars who take the position that if we simply teach the

Bible that our congregations will mature and becoming the loving and holy people God wants them to be. As such, they advocate that the only way to teach the Bible is to teach it exegetically. I respectfully disagree and take the position that a dutiful pastor will teach and preach with a good balance of both exegetical and topical sermons. My belief is based on one of Paul's instructions to Titus.

In *Titus 2:1*, Paul writes to his son in the faith, "But you are to proclaim *things consistent with* sound teaching."[42] (Emphasis mine) As I read this verse, Paul makes a distinction here between "sound doctrine" and "things consistent with" sound doctrine. In other words, we must teach our congregations the Bible as God's Word, but we must also teach on subject matters that may not be expressly included in the Bible. The latter subjects must, of course, be taught in such a way that they are consistent with God's Word. The Bible does not, for example, provide us with any detailed instruction for how to best manage our household finances. The local church can and should, however, teach our respective congregations principles relating to finance management that are consistent with God's Word (such as making sure that household budgets account for giving to others).

If you are called to become a pastor, or if you are reading this book in an attempt to determine whether you are being properly served by your pastor, then you must give heed to Paul's teaching on the preeminence and priority of the Holy Scriptures in pastoral ministry. His constant use of the phrase "sound doctrine" points to a specific and identified body of work – the Holy Bible – as being the correct standard for how the follower of Jesus Christ must live and conduct himself before the church and others.

Now that we have looked at the pastor's call and that which has been communicated by God, let's turn to the final force in a pastor's ministry – his character. Before we do, however, let's look at how His Call and The

Communicated interact in the model I am building to reflect the power-filled pastor (See, Figure 2).

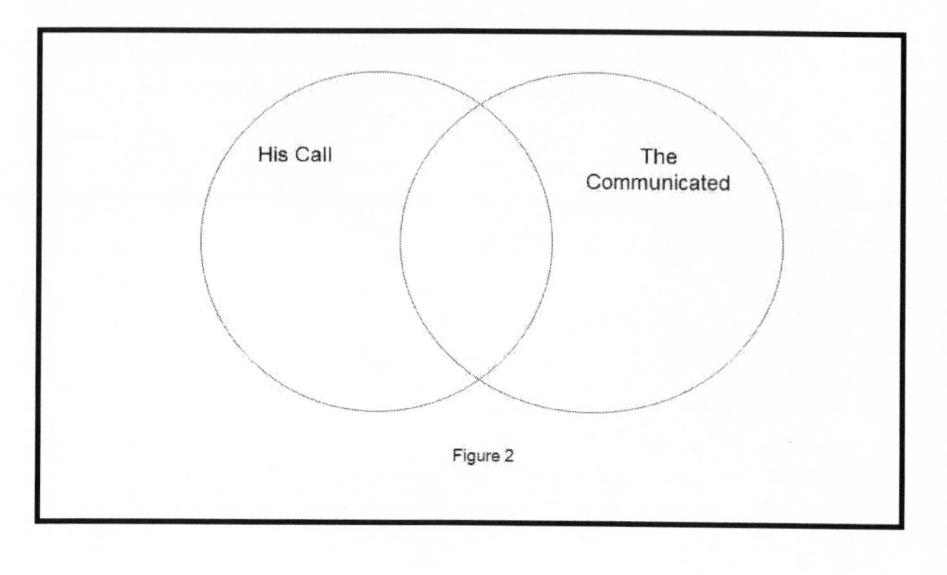

Figure 2

Questions

1. If you are currently a pastor, is the teaching of God's Word your central concern and priority? Are you caring for your congregation by feeding them a steady diet of "sound doctrine"?

2. Given the current climate in the United States, have you backed down from using phrases like "The Bible says" or "God's Word" when referring to the Bible? Does your teaching reflect the belief that the Bible is the inerrant and inspired Word of God?

3. If you are a pastor, how would you and your congregation answer the questions posed on pp. 28?

Recommended Reading

1. John MacArthur, ed., *The Scripture Cannot Be Broken*. Wheaton, IL: Crossway, 2015.

2. Bobby Jamieson, *Sound Doctrine: How a Church Grows in the Love and Holiness of God*. Wheaton, IL: Crossway, 2013.

4 HIS CHARACTER

All you have to do is insert the phrase "fallen pastors" into Google's search engine to get hundreds of hits on news stories and websites detailing the many ways pastors derail their respective callings through a sinful act or series of acts. In committing everything from adultery to financial fraud to mistreating church staff and volunteers through emotional and verbal abuse, too many pastors have undone the preaching of God's Word and have brought shame upon God's church through their acts of sin. Worse yet, these sins often lead people to walk away from both the church and their faith.

Paul emphasizes twice in our key passage the need for Timothy to guard his personal character as a man and a pastor. In verse 12 he writes, for instance, "Don't let anyone despise your youth, but set an example for the believers in speech, in conduct, in love, in faith, and in purity." Pastors are expected to behave in a manner that provides an example for those disciples of Jesus Christ that the Lord has assigned to their personal care. On this issue, well-known pastor John MacArthur writes that a pastor must

> live in such a holy manner that his preaching would never be in contradiction to his lifestyle, that the pastor's indiscretions never bring shame on the ministry, and that the shepherd's hypocrisy not undermine the flock's confidence in the ministry of God.[43]

On this same topic of a pastor's personal holiness, Donald Whitney writes:

> Ministers must model godliness to God's flock, providing them with a pattern of

holiness they can see and follow. Yes, God primarily calls pastors to preach His Word to His people, for by this means they will understand God's truth about holiness. But the pastor should also model by his life and piety how to apply God's truth about holiness in everyday life.[44]

In his second mention on this topic in our key passage, Paul writes to Timothy, "Pay close attention to your life and your teaching; persevere in these things, for in doing this you will save both yourself and your hearers."[45] This strikes to the very core of what often causes many people to leave churches – the double standard many pastors demonstrate by teaching one thing, while living quite another. There are two crucial points Paul makes regarding this instruction of the pastor's need to watch his character and to make sure that it comports with his teaching. The first is that such consistency requires perseverance. It doesn't just happen. It requires our constantly examining ourselves to make sure that we are living in a manner that reflects our teaching and what we should be believing as pastors and as disciples of Jesus Christ. The second point Paul makes is that consistency between our walk and our talk is necessary for both our salvation and the salvation of others. Regarding our own salvation, the consistency regarding our own walk goes to the issue of persevering in the faith as an outward manifestation of that salvation.[46] Regarding the salvation of others, we may discourage others in their faith by falling into sin. Whether we like it or not, the salvation of others depends on the integrity of our walk. So what should that walk look like?

Paul is actually very specific in his advice to Timothy. He says that, as pastors, we should be setting an example in how we use our words, in how we behave, in how we love others, in how we live out our faith, and in maintaining our sexual purity. Let's begin with our speech.

Watch Your Mouth

The Bible has much to say about how Christians should talk to others and the appropriate topics of conversation for those of us who are disciples of Jesus Christ. We know from *Proverbs 12:6*, for example, that "The words of the wicked are a deadly ambush, but the speech of the upright rescues them." *Colossians 4:6* says, "Let your speech always be gracious, seasoned with salt, so that you may know how you should answer each person." How we speak to people and what we say matters to God.

How is all this relevant to the pastor, especially today? We live in a time when, at least in the United States, humor and sarcasm have taken a prominent place in our public discourse. Our society seems to value and praise those quick-witted individuals who can deftly respond to others in a snarky and demeaning manner. There's one pastor whose teaching I have enjoyed for years, but have stopped listening to him because he's become downright mean in his criticism of those he disagrees with on theological matters.

There is one verse that I believe captures the gold standard for disciples of Jesus Christ when it comes to our speech. That verse is found at *Ephesians 4:29*, which says, "No foul language should come from your mouth, but only what is good for building up someone in need, so that it gives grace to those who hear." I actually like the 1984 edition of the New International Version better, which says, "Do not let any unwholesome talk come out of your mouths, but only what is helpful for building others up according to their needs, that it may benefit those who listen."

The Greek word for "foul language" in the CSB or "unwholesome" in the NIV84 can be translated as "rotten, worn out, unfit for use, worthless, and bad."[47] There are two important lessons taught by this verse. The first is that our speech can be useless and destructive in its effect, even when we don't intend it to be. Christians have the obligation, therefore, to understand the power of the tongue. This is why in *Proverbs 18:21*, the Word of God says, "Death and life are in the power of the tongue, and those who love it will eat its fruit." James, the brother of Jesus, has a much more powerful discourse on the power of the tongue to destroy. He wrote to the Jewish Christians scattered by the assassination of Stephen,

> And the tongue is a fire. The tongue, a world of unrighteousness, is placed among our members. It stains the whole body, sets the course of life on fire, and is itself set on fire by hell. Every kind of animal, bird, reptile, and fish is tamed and has been tamed by humankind, but no one can tame the tongue. It is a restless evil, full of deadly poison.[48]

We are urged to control our speech because of the potential harm it can do to others, especially to the community of faith.

The second lesson taught to us by *Ephesians 4:29* is that we have a choice in how we speak and that we must choose to build others up by the use of our speech. And remember that even our Lord and Savior, Jesus Christ, saw fit to warn us about the use of our words. In *Matthew 12:36-37*, he said, "I tell you that on the day of judgment people will have to account for every careless word they speak. For by your words you will be acquitted, and by your words you will be condemned." And even the Apostle Peter wrote to the church that you should be "ready at any time to give a defense to anyone who asks you for a reason for your hope that is in you. Yet do it with gentleness and respect …".[49] Even when dealing with non-believers, we must control our speech so that Jesus's love is experienced through what we say and how we say it.

So how is all of this significant for the pastor? We are expected to both practice and model the use of the tongue for those we encounter in our congregation and elsewhere. This is why Paul instructs Timothy to set an example "in speech" – pastors have a higher obligation to use their speech in a way that builds people up. This doesn't mean avoiding the confrontation of sin, the discussion of unpleasant topics, or forsaking the confrontation of false doctrine. But it does mean that we should avoid destructive speech patterns in our preaching and conversation, such as sarcasm, snarkiness, or deprecating humor.

Of course, it goes without saying that this aspect of our lives has been complicated by the technological extension of our tongues through the creation and development of social media. In fact, our world has seen so many careers and lives ruined by inconsiderate or poorly written messages posted on Twitter or Facebook that books are now being written on the issue. In one such book – "Before You Hit Send" – author Emerson Eggerichs warns,

> Social media means what it says: it is *social.* World Wide Web means worldwide. Our methods of communication today allow our message to be broadcast to potentially millions, from Auckland, New Zealand, to Oakland, California …
>
> Every day we have the potential of both verbal and written blunders. It makes no difference if we are talking to a stranger over a meat counter, chatting on a cell phone with

the service department, or sending an e-mail to a coworker; we can miscommunicate and people can get the wrong idea.[50]

As pastors, we must consider that the ability of our speech to reach others is vastly multiplied by social media platforms. If we don't carefully think about what we repost, we can do great damage to others by encouraging them to engage in negative feelings like bitterness or contempt. We can also bring great shame and embarrassment to our church or the greater community of disciples by posting an insensitive or poorly considered message. I must sadly confess that I have not always been thoughtful about what I post in an era where one misstatement or a message posted in anger can lead to great harm to others and the Lord's reputation. I am sharing this warning not as one who has mastered the practice, but one who has struggled with it. Regardless, the *Ephesians 4:29* golden rule applies to the use of social media as well – do not use unwholesome words, but only communicate that which will build others up.

Our Conduct and Our Purity

Even though conduct and purity are listed separately in our key passage, I am going to write about them together for two reasons. First, when all is said and done, issues of purity are eventually manifested as conduct. When a pastor opens the door to sexual sin through his thought life, those thoughts can and often do eventually lead to fornication, adultery, or even a pornography addiction. Second, there are two types of conduct that continue to happen at churches all over the world and usually lead to the downfall of a pastor and pain for those he has been called to shepherd – financial improprieties or sexual misconduct.

The word "conduct," in *1 Timothy 4:12* is the Greek word *anastrophē*, which means "way of life" or "behavior."[51] It refers to one's mode of life or, more importantly, his consistent lifestyle. Because a pastor is a teaching elder, one need simply look to Paul's list of elder qualifications in *1 Timothy 3* and *Titus 1* to see what Paul means when he teaches Timothy to set an example "in conduct."[52] Those qualifications, as listed by Paul to Timothy are as follows:

> An overseer, therefore, must be above reproach, the husband of one wife, self-controlled, sensible, respectable, hospitable, able to teach, not an excessive drinker, not a bully but gentle, not quarrelsome, not greedy. He must manage his own household competently and have his children under control with all dignity. (If anyone does not know how to manage his own household, how will he take care of God's church?) He must not be a new convert, or he might become conceited and incur the same condemnation as the devil. Furthermore, he must have a good reputation among outsiders, so that he does not fall into disgrace and the devil's trap.[53]

The key standard in this passage is that an elder must be "above reproach." When joined together with Paul's teaching that Timothy must set an example for others "in conduct," we can appreciate that the pastor must be careful to guard his lifestyle in such a way as to reflect a commitment to holiness in the Lord.

The Greek word for "above reproach," which can also be translated "blameless," is *anepilambanō*. Wuest explains that the word means, "one who cannot be laid hold upon."[54] The idea here is that pastors must live life in such a way that others cannot truthfully raise an objection or accusation against a pastor, or his conduct, that would bring shame to our Lord and Savior, Jesus Christ, or His Gospel. S. J. Robinson explains it this way: "No one should be able to point the finger of accusation at a leader justly because of serious inconsistencies in his life."[55] If you are a pastor, be aware – whether you believe it is fair or not, congregations are watching us and we can cause many to lose their way or fall away from the faith because we have failed to live a holy life.

NOTE TO CHURCH LEADERS

While pastors and church leaders are to be held to the standard of being "above reproach" (1 Timothy 3:2), congregations and other leaders should avoid the temptation to translate this standard in their minds as "perfection." When a pastor commits a sin, elders, trustees, and congregations are often quick to fire him without showing that pastor the grace that God showed all of us by delivering His Son for our sins. Allow me to submit for your consideration that there are times, when a pastor sins, that you should consider restoring him. Can't we be an example to our congregations in how we humbly ask for forgiveness and submit to the restoration and leading of our elders and leaders? Is there a better way for you to teach your congregation about grace than to let them see you extend it to a fallen pastor? Granted, there may be sins that prohibit restoration to pastoral ministry, but be careful not to destroy someone's call to ministry when it can be saved through grace.

Loving Others

Of course, our speech and conduct should not be a problem if we are consistently motivated in our actions by true Christian love. In our book's key passage, Paul instructs Timothy to be an example "in love." The word love, as used in this passage, is the Greek word *agapē* – love that is given away without expecting anything in return. It is the same love Paul writes about to the Ephesians when he tells them, "Therefore, be imitators of God, as dearly loved children, and walk in *love*, as Christ also loved us and gave himself for us, a sacrificial and fragrant offering to God."[56] *Agapē* love is the standard of love for every disciple of Jesus Christ, but especially the pastor.

Earlier in his letter to Timothy, Paul gave the ingredients for how a pastor obtains this love for those in his congregation. In the very first chapter of his letter to Timothy, Paul writes, "Now the goal of our instruction is love that comes from a pure heart, a good conscience, and a sincere faith."[57] In other words, this *agapē* love flows from the pastor that has a pure heart, a good conscience, and a sincere faith. The word "good" here is the Greek word *agathos*. In explaining the significance of this word, Kenneth Wuest quotes Hermann Cremer as writing,

> The word expresses in its use, a recognition alike simple and full, that the thing spoken of is perfect in its kind, so as to produce pleasure, satisfaction, and a sense of well-being. The fundamental conception of the word is that of well-being, pleasure. Good is existence which is perfect and promotes perfection.
>
> The transference of this conception to the sphere of morals was easy. Since that is *good*

which, after its kind, is perfect, the sphere of good at once fundamentally limits itself to that which is as in general a thing should be, and thus the word becomes synonymous with *dikaios* (δικαιος) (righteous), observing divine and human laws, upright, virtuous, keeping the commands of God.[58]

A good conscience, therefore, belongs to the disciple and pastor who knows that he is walking as God commands, in a way that is holy and righteous. The reader should note that though the quality of a good conscience is mentioned here in the context of developing the ability to demonstrate *agapē* love, that it also shows the interrelatedness of all the qualities Paul lists in verse 12 of our key passage. A pastor who watches his conduct and purity is developing the ability to show Christian love to his congregation and the world because his conscience is clear as he is ministering in the power of God's love and His approval.

Equally important to developing the ability to demonstrate *agapē* love is the quality of a sincere faith. The word "sincere" in *1 Timothy 1:5* is the Greek word *anypokritos*, which literally means "without hypocrisy." The person with sincere faith is one whose faith is genuine; there is no pretense, frivolity, or show in this person's faith. A pastor with a sincere faith is one who ministers to his congregation with total and complete assurance that he can do what God says he can do. In fact, this sincere faith is such an important quality to possess that Paul expressly includes it in his verse 12 list.

Living Out Our Faith

Finally, Paul tells Timothy that he must set an example "in faith." This reference, of course, is to pastors setting an example for their respective congregations on how to live out our faith in practice. If you are already a pastor, here are some questions to ask yourself: If my congregation had access to a camera that followed me all day long, what kind of example would I be in reading the Bible? Praying and meditating? Practicing the spiritual disciplines like silence, solitude, fasting, and worship?[59] What kind of example am I setting in how I treat others?

Now allow me to inform you of something – your congregation does not need such a camera. If you are failing to practice your faith, your congregation will know. How? By your preaching. An anemic prayer and devotional life will make itself apparent in the your preaching, both in its poor quality as well as in its failure to yield fruit. In addition, our preaching often reveals our attitude toward people and, as a result, our congregation will often feel our contempt for them. The opposite is also true – a pastor with a life steeped in Bible study, devotional reading, prayer, meditation, and the spiritual disciplines, will be a powerful preacher of God's Word and that power will be demonstrated in the number of souls won to Jesus Christ and in a congregation that is clicking on all cylinders when it comes to the giving of their time, talent, and treasure and by the way they relate to one another along with their attitude towards those outside of the church; that congregation will know they are loved by its pastor.

And so there we have it. According to Paul's instruction in *1 Timothy 4:12-16*, the pastor needs to access three forces to have a successful life and ministry – His Call, The Communicated, and His Character (See, Figure 3). In fact, all of these are critical not only to the pastor's success and well-being, but also for the benefit of the pastor's congregation. Whitney explains it this way:

> The church will never rise spiritually above the level of its leadership. A people will never become godlier than their pastor.

The pastor is the pacesetter; that's what it means to be an example ... pastors must show the church what Christlikeness looks like here and now. Christians should get their cues of what God-honoring speech is from their pastor. They will know what Christlike conduct is by watching his conduct. He should strive to be the most like Jesus "in love, in faith, in purity" and in all Christlike qualities so that they will see how they need to grow in them. Whatever the pastor wants his people to live out, he must do it the most.[60]

But what happens if the pastor doesn't access all three simultaneously? What happens if he leans on His Call and The Communicated, but ignores His Character? The rest of this book will present a fuller model that explains what happens when a pastor operates in only two of the forces and not all three simultaneously. I will also end the book by discussing how to maintain the three forces, warn you about what can drain the three forces, and finally close with some thoughts about technology and its effects on ministry and church work.

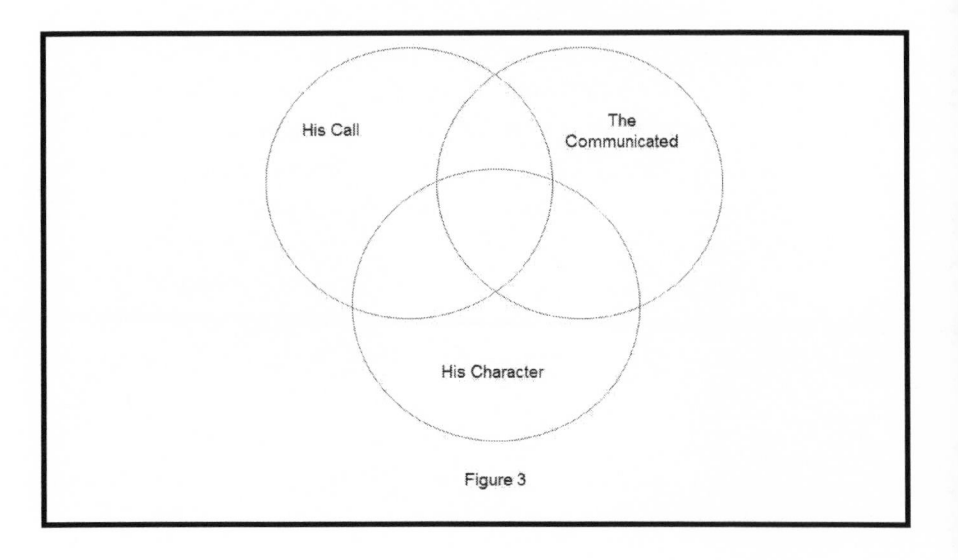

Figure 3

Questions

1. Can your congregation honestly look to you as a good example when it comes to their speech, conduct, love, faith, and purity? Are there any activities that you carry out when no one is looking that would cast doubt on your maturity and sincerity as a disciple of Jesus Christ?

2. How much thought do you give to your jokes and sarcastic remarks when you preach? Has anyone ever expressed being hurt or offended? Does your preaching come off as loving or judgmental?

3. If the Apostle Paul were to spend time with you, would he say that you have a pure heart, a good conscience, and a sincere faith?

Recommended Reading

1. Emerson Eggerichs. *Before You Hit Send.* Nashville, TN: W Publishing Group, 2017.

2. Skye Jethani. *Immeasurable: Reflections on the Soul of Ministry in the Age of Church, Inc.* Chicago, IL: Moody Publishers, 2017.

5 THE NEED FOR ALL THREE FORCES

As we have seen so far, the pastor's ability to minister in power and in might flows from his possessing the three forces Paul lists in our key passage. A pastor must simultaneously lean on his calling from God, on the Holy Scriptures inspired by God, and on the integrity of his character to fully thrive in ministry (See, Figure 4).

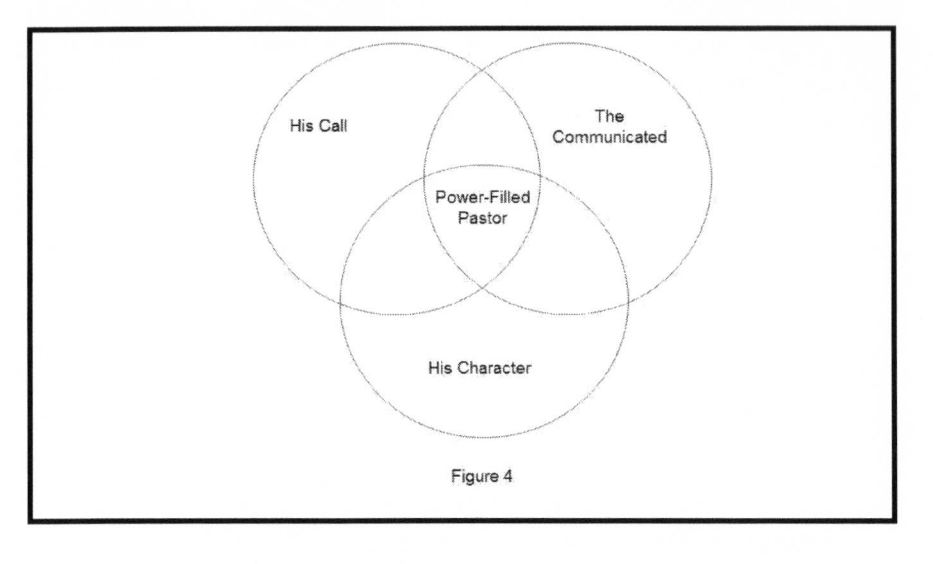

Figure 4

Given the availability of Paul's teaching to Timothy, however, regarding a pastor's call, the communicated, and the need for a pastor to keep his character, why do so many pastors fail? Why do so many pastors succumb to the temptations of adulterous behavior or financial impropriety? Why do so many pastors become so harsh and legalistic in their shepherding of congregations? Why are there so many pastors who fail to produce fruit, leading anemic ministries that don't grow or provide any indication of God's power? Why is the church in the United States of America losing its voice in the marketplace of public opinion and seen as increasingly irrelevant by the young and the influential?

While there are many sound theories and arguments being offered to explain the state of the church today, we must consider that as pastors go so goes the church. This is why Paul emphasized to Timothy the need to insure the consistency between our walk and our doctrine, as shepherds representing Jesus Christ, because "in doing this you will save both yourself and your hearers."[61] In other words, pastors are tasked with leading the church in such a way that, through our teaching and our living, we can lead people to salvation and holiness. So how are pastors falling short?

Pastors are failing because they are not learning and practicing the three God-given forces presented by Paul in our key passage. More specifically, many pastors do not have the three God-given forces working actively and simultaneously in their respective lives and ministries. One pastor may have his call and his character, but not the communicated. Another pastor may have the communicated and his call, but not his character. In the end, the power-filled pastor must have all three forces working together and at the same time to experience the fullness of God's power in his life and ministry.

What happens when a pastor has only two of the forces operating? What are the consequences of this deficiency? The remainder of this chapter will be dedicated to presenting the consequences of a pastor's failure to walk in these three gifts. Each explanation will be reflected in the model that has been built throughout this book as we specifically learn about the three pastors that fall short – the Pharisaic Pastor, the Phony Pastor, and the Permissive Pastor.

His Character and The Communicated – The Pharisaic Pastor

What happens when a pastor, in carrying out his ministry responsibilities, leans on his character and the communicated, but is not operating in, or is dependent on, his call? What kind of pastor will he become? A pastor who has a great command of the Bible, whose character reflects great integrity and holiness, but who fails to operate under his calling often becomes a "Pharisaic Pastor" (See, Figure 5).

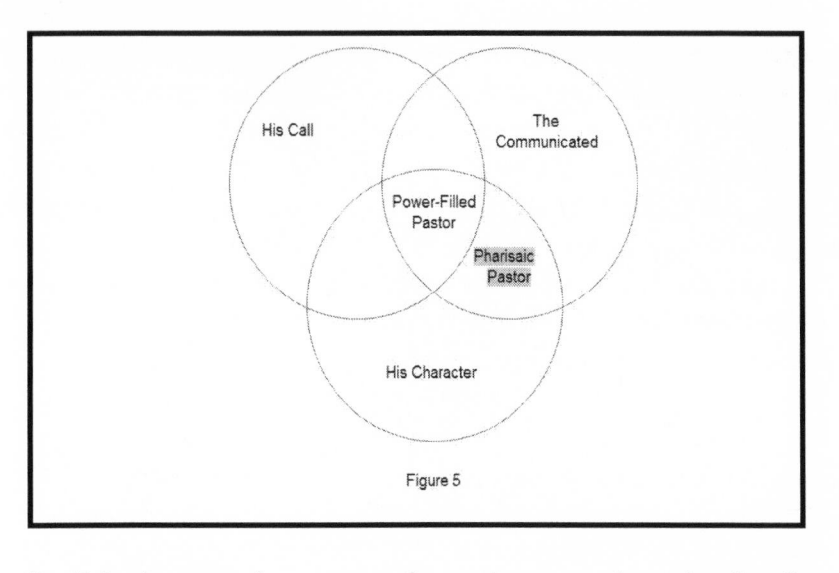

Figure 5

In John's gospel account, he twice mentions in the first chapter that Jesus came in grace *and* in truth.[62] The challenge with pastors that operate only in their character and in the communicated is that they live and minister in the truth part of that equation, but act as though grace doesn't exist. They tend to teach the Bible as a rulebook and are quite legalistic in their attitude toward their congregations and the world. Their preaching is often harsh and they are quite condemning of people who don't agree with their interpretation of Scripture and of people who don't know the Lord.

Your failure, as a pastor, to walk in your call is significant because it means you have decided to minister without the Lord's power. God's power, which operates in the believer's life through the indwelling of the Holy Spirit, not only provides for our ability to teach the

Scriptures but it also gives us two important qualities that are needed as a shepherd of God's people – grace and humility. Why do I believe this? Because humanity's tendency, when left to the desires of the flesh, is to judge others harshly.

The Apostle Paul addressed this tendency to judge in his letter to the Romans. The first time we see it is in Chapter 2, when he points out the hypocrisy of those who judge others while committing the same sins as those they are judging. Paul warns them, "every one of you who judges is without excuse. For when you judge another, you condemn yourself, since you, the judge, do the same things."[63] And later in Chapter 14, Paul address those situations when Christians differ over "disputed matters", by writing,

> But you, why do you judge your brother or sister? Or you, why do you despise your brother and sister? For we all stand before the judgment seat of God ... So then, let us pursue what promotes peace and what builds up one another.[64]

The truth is, even as blood-bought, born again, baptized believers in Jesus Christ, we all struggle with the inclination to judge others and the pastor, as a Christian, does not escape this tendency. And how do I know the pastor struggles with this sinful desire to judge? Because of Paul's advice to Timothy about loving and not arguing.

There are two specific aspects of Paul's advice to Timothy that informs me that pastors struggle with this tendency to judge. The first is Paul's reminder to Timothy that the purpose of his instruction "is love that comes from a pure heart, a good conscience, and a sincere faith."[65] If we as pastors attempt to teach God's Word without this kind of love we can easily fall into the temptation of being harsh taskmasters, seeing our congregations as people who need to be lectured and disciplined, rather than seeing them as souls that need to be fed, loved, and guided. We often tend to forget that when Jesus restored Peter to ministry, he instructed him to feed and tend his sheep.[66] As Jared Wilson correctly reminds us, "You won't feed the sheep unless you love the sheep."[67]

The second aspect of Paul's advice that shows pastors struggle with the tendency to judge is his constant reminder that pastors should not argue. In his second letter to Timothy, for example, Paul writes, "But reject foolish and ignorant disputes, because you know that they breed quarrels. The Lord's servant must not quarrel, but must be gentle to everyone, able to teach, and patient, instructing his opponents with gentleness."[68] And even to Titus, Paul wrote, "But avoid foolish debates, genealogies, quarrels, and disputes about the law, because they are unprofitable and worthless."[69] My point here is that this tendency to argue comes from a spirit of judgment and our need often to "correct" people who don't think like we do or act like we think they should. Once again, this instruction is not about whether we, as pastors, should confront false doctrine or sin. Rather it is about *how* we do it. Our ability to refrain from judging, and to actively show the love of Jesus Christ to others, relies on our standing in the same grace that Jesus showed us when he died on the cross. Accessing that grace, as a pastor, means standing in our calling and the power of the Holy Spirit to help us have Jesus's heart to those we shepherd and instruct.

His Call and The Communicated – The Phony Pastor

A pastor who is only operating in his call to ministry and in the communicated, but not in the integrity of his character, often becomes the "Phony Pastor" (See, Figure 6). This is a pastor who has a confirmed call to preach the gospel and who has used his gifts to become an effective teacher of the Scriptures, but whose personal life does not reflect the standard of holiness he has been called to demonstrate in his daily living.

I had dinner with a friend once who shared with me the horrible circumstances that led him to leave a church where he was serving as an associate pastor. That church held a revival one year where several visiting pastors were to preach over a period of five days. In anticipation of this revival, these pastors were gathered in a meeting and my friend decided to bring them food so they could eat as they planned this event. As he served them, they were having a conversation he never thought he would hear in a church. These so-called "pastors" were sharing tips with one another on how to cheat on their wives without being caught. Can you believe it? Men called to be Christ's ambassadors, to represent the Kingdom of God, and to preach His Gospel of salvation and redemption – they are committing adultery and encouraging others to do the same.

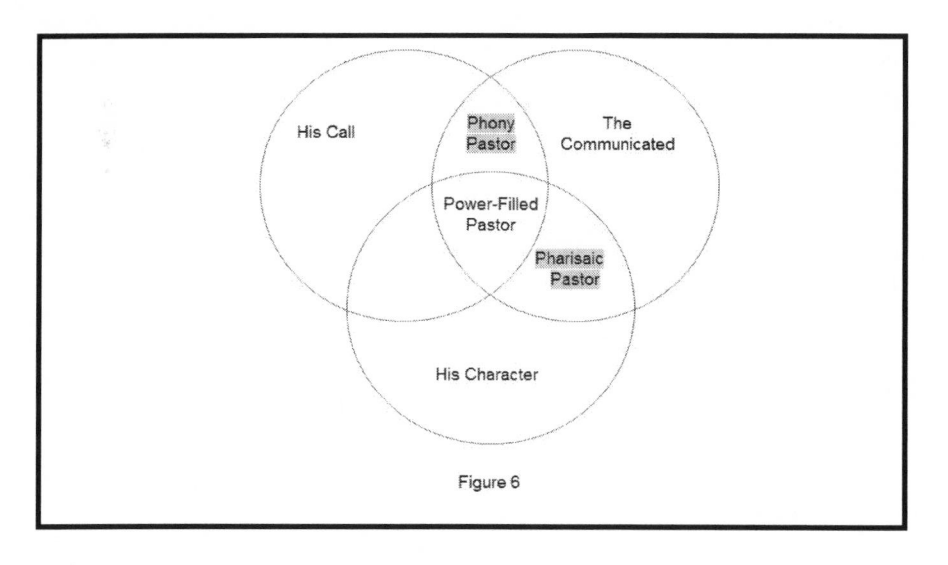

Figure 6

Do you now understand why there are people who can't stand Christians or the idea of going to church? Can you see why pastors and the church have lost our collective voice in the marketplace of ideas? A pastor who fails to guard his character does not just ruin his own credibility, but he undermines the credibility of the very One who sent him and of the very Gospel itself. Once again, this is why Paul instructed Timothy, "Pay close attention to your life and your teaching; persevere in these things, for in doing this you will save both yourself and your hearers."[70]

There are two other reasons I would give pastors for keeping the integrity of their character. First, God's judgment for such behavior, on the part of those He has called to be pastors, will be severe. James the brother of Jesus warns, for example, "Not many of you should become teachers, my brothers, for you know that we who teach will be judged with greater strictness."[71] The very calling to become a pastor imposes on us a higher standard of living and our Heavenly Father will hold us accountable to that higher standard. And God has been consistent in insisting on the truth that pastors will be judged severely for their sins, for this standard for pastors carries over from the Old Testament. In prophesying against Israel, for instance, Hosea had harsh words for the priests who failed to lead the people to righteousness. He is recorded as saying,

> But let no one dispute; let no one argue, for my case is against you priests. You will stumble by day; the prophet will also stumble with you by night. And I will destroy your mother. My people are destroyed for lack of knowledge, I will reject you from serving as my priest. Since you have forgotten the law of your God, I will forget yours sons.[72]

God equates our sin to our forgetting his law and to

failing to teach his people the law so that they too are living in sin. If you are a pastor living in continual sin, you are calling God's judgment upon you as a certainty.

Second, God warns us through His Word that no person, even a pastor, can get away with sin. In Luke, Jesus promises that, "nothing is concealed that won't be revealed, and nothing hidden that won't be made known and brought to light."[73] All that we do in secret will one day be revealed to all. And in *Hebrews 4:13*, we are warned that "No creature is hidden from him, but all things are naked and exposed to the eyes of him to whom we must give an account." Imagine yourself "naked and exposed" before your congregation and your community. How many pastors carried on affairs for years before those affairs became known to their family and congregation? How many lives and churches have been destroyed because of such sin? And even if you could get away with such sin before humanity, the Lord will know about that sin and you will be called to account for it on the Day of Judgment. What then? God forbid that you would one day stand in the Lord's presence and say to him – "Lord, didn't I proclaim your Gospel and preach Your Word?" – only to hear Him respond, "I never knew you. Depart from me, you lawbreaker!"[74]

In the end, your call and your ability to teach the Scriptures are not sufficient by themselves in carrying out your ministry responsibilities. If you have been called to be a pastor, God has decided to entrust human souls to your care and those souls depend on you to not only hear the Gospel of Jesus Christ for salvation, but to also be led to holiness by your teaching and your example.

His Call and His Character – The Permissive Pastor

I personally know pastors that have an obvious calling to preach the Gospel and who are people of great character and integrity. They are wonderful individuals who I love and believe in, people who I trust to be around my wife and my children. But I have one concern for them as pastors – they have adopted and expressed views suggesting that the Bible is somehow flawed or, in some cases, they have outright denied the inerrancy of the Holy Scriptures. The pastor who leans on his calling and his character, but fails to operate in the communicated as the inspired, inerrant, and authoritative Word of God, is the "Permissive Pastor" (See, Figure 7).

The Permissive Pastor does not fully believe that the Bible is the inspired, inerrant Word of God. They have adopted many of the 20th century theories that give later dates to many of the Bible's books and often question whether Jesus actually said much of the teaching directly attributed to him by the Gospel writers. They often dismiss significant teachings from the Bible as being culturally irrelevant to our modern situation. And to what end? We often have pastors teaching a gospel that is no gospel at all and they lead churches full of people whose lives look no different than the world.

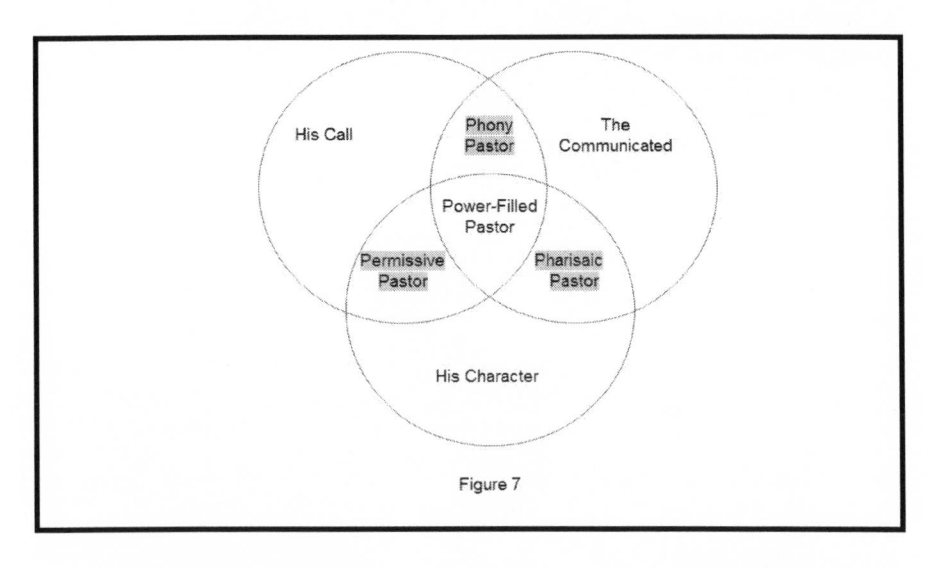

Figure 7

Permissive Pastors can often be recognized by the extremity of what they teach. They will teach, for example, that it is important for us to help our fellow humans (such as caring for the homeless or welcoming refugees), but spend no time teaching on personal holiness as God defines it in His Word. The churches led by these pastors have much to say about the politics of our time, but their opinions are grounded in the world's ideas of morality rather than what God has communicated in His Word. They reflect the need people have, in our current times, to have both God and their personal preferences. It is in this spirit, for example, that they confidently declare that one can be a Christian and simultaneously live in a so-called same-sex marriage. There are other pastors who spend much time teaching that God wants you to be blessed and prosperous, but their teaching will lead you to believe that the Bible is silent on trials and suffering. In the end, I call them Permissive Pastors because they teach a gospel that leads us to the lie that God will accept you on your terms and that He expects nothing from you in regards to holiness. The Permissive Pastor is the one desired and accepted by congregations that Paul warned Timothy about when he wrote,

> For the time will come when people will not tolerate sound doctrine, but according to their own desires, will multiply teachers for themselves because they have an itch to hear what they want to hear. They will turn away from hearing the truth and will turn aside to myths.[75]

In the end, such a gospel is no gospel at all because it cannot and does not lead to an abiding, saving faith in Jesus Christ that results in holiness as it is defined by God's Word.

Paul follows up his warning to Timothy, about the people who resist sound doctrine, by writing, "But as for you, exercise self-control in everything, endure hardship, do the work of an evangelist, fulfill your ministry."[76] The fulfillment of a pastor's ministry is to preach the Bible faithfully as the inspired, inerrant, and authoritative Word of God. And to do so while watching his own walk as a disciple of Jesus Christ.

Questions

1. Does your preaching and your attitude reflect a legalistic attitude on your part? What if God had that same attitude toward you when you first answered Jesus Christ's call to salvation? As a pastor, where do you stand in the balance between grace and truth?

2. Do you have a secret life that your congregation and family don't know about? If Jesus projected your thoughts and hidden life on a screen before your congregation, would they continue to have you as their pastor?

3. Is your preaching guided by the truth that God's Word is inspired and inerrant? Or is your preaching guided by what society thinks is right and moral?

Recommended Reading

1. Jason K. Allen, ed. *Portraits of a Pastor*. Chicago, IL: Moody Publishers, 2017.

2. Jared C. Wilson. *The Pastor's Justification: Applying the Work of Christ in Your Life and Ministry*. Wheaton, IL: Crossway, 2013.

6 MAINTAINING THE THREE FORCES

One of the most influential books I have ever read is Stephen Covey's "Seven Habits of Highly Effective People." I read it when I was still practicing law and it helped me to increase my effectiveness as a lawyer and eventually as the head of a government agency. I immediately thought of the Covey's seventh habit – "Sharpening Your Saw" – as I sat down to write this chapter and the one following.

The idea of sharpening your saw is simply recognizing the need for the care and maintenance of yourself to continue your effectiveness in whatever role you play in both your professional and personal life. For the professional athlete it means eating a sensible diet, stretching exercises and body maintenance (such as massages), and working with trainers to keep their bodies honed for action. The teacher needs to use the summer to rest and to study so that she continues to be able to build into her students. The lawyer needs to regularly take continuing legal education classes to stay informed about the latest changes in the law. Every adult needs to engage in specific activities designed to maximize their potential in whatever field they are working and serving in.

The pastor is no exception to this reality. For the individual called to Christian ministry, specifically as a pastor, the need to adopt the habit of sharpening the saw has a twofold consequence – first, the need for the pastor to maintain the three forces in his life and, second, the need for a pastor to guard against whatever might drain him and the three forces. In his book – "Zeal Without Burnout" – author Christopher Ash reminds us that there is a difference between godly sacrifice and burnout.[77] The focus in this chapter will be on engaging in activities and adopting practices to maintain the three forces and Chapter 7 will be about avoiding those things that drain the three forces.

Maintaining the Call

Because our calling as pastors flows from our walking in God's will and the enablement of the Holy Spirit to exercise the gifts we have been given to shepherd God's people, sharpening this part of our saw is about our need to be connected to the Lord. I am specifically talking about the pastor's devotional life and his intentional efforts to stay connected to God. We cannot effectively minister to God's people unless we have allowed the Holy Spirit to first minister to us. Hence, it is critical that the pastor design his schedule to allow him for time to be with the Lord and to be in His Word.

There are many books that will present you with a comprehensive discussion on this subject.[78] My goal here is to simply share a few true and tested activities that will allow a pastor to walk in his calling effectively, over an extended period of time, if he practices them.

Daily prayer and devotional reading: A pastor's daily time with the Lord is a lifeline for his health and strength as he seeks to carry out his ministry duties. We can spend so much time caring for others that we neglect our own spiritual health. This is why it is critical to make sure that we start our day by praying and reading the Bible.

I want to emphasize that this reading of the Bible is not about studying in preparation for teaching others. Prime and Begg remind us, for example, that "Before ever we are shepherds and teachers, we are first and foremost sons of God, and our spiritual life demands to be nurtured."[79] The reading of the Bible I am discussing here, therefore, is about you getting God's Word for yourself. It is about allowing God's Word to be our connection to the very presence of God.

Most pastors I know would tell you that making this a part of your morning ritual is most helpful. A thriving ministry means that you are probably thrown right into the fire once you walk out of your front door. Praying and reading devotionally before you leave the house in the morning will help you to stay centered as you encounter all that life, ministry, and the evil one will throw at you during the day. As a practical matter, if your home life is not currently conducive to doing your devotions at home, set up your office calendar so that your appointments don't start until Noon. Then try to go straight into your office, lock the door, and ask the Lord to meet you there.

Spiritual disciplines: Part of walking in your call and attending to your spiritual well-being is about making time to be with God alone. This is why I urge pastors, as I do all disciples of Jesus Christ, to regularly practice some of the spiritual disciplines. I say "some" of the spiritual disciplines because there are quite a few, according to authors like Dallas Willard, and there's no way that any Christian, including the pastor, will have the time or energy to practice all of them.[80] That being said, I do want to emphasize some of the ones I believe can be most helpful.

Let me begin by recognizing that prayer and reading God's Word devotionally count as spiritual disciplines. So if you can get yourself into the habit of practicing these every day you are setting yourself up to have a close relationship with our Lord. I will add two more that I believe can be quite helpful in helping us to guard our relationship with the Lord – solitude and silence.

In reading the gospels, have you ever noticed how often Jesus goes off to be alone with the Father? There are at least eight mentions of Jesus going off to pray alone to places like a mountain (*Matthew 14:23*; *Mark 6:46*; *Luke 6:12*) or the wilderness (*Luke 5:16*). Mark writes in one place that the Lord simply went away to a secluded or deserted place (*Mark 1:35*). And Luke specifically wrote about Jesus, "Yet he *often* withdrew to deserted places and prayed."[81] I have always been particularly intrigued by the fact that Luke makes more mention of Jesus going off to pray alone than the other Gospel writers. Why? Because Luke is the only Gospel writer that is a physician. It makes sense that a man dedicated to the physical well-being of others would pay particular attention to the Lord's practice of going off to be alone in prayer and to recognize the health value of this practice. This time alone with the Lord is necessary and beneficial to our overall well-being. As pastors, we should follow the Lord's lead.

Personal retreats: One of the ways that a pastor can make time for the spiritual disciplines and to avoid some of the drains I discuss in the next chapter is to take short retreats to be refreshed and renewed. This is especially true if you are the lead pastor of a large or growing and dynamic ministry. I am talking about getting away to a location separate and apart from the church so that you decrease the chance that you will see anyone who knows you and you can devote your time to activities that refresh and renew you.

While I am not the lead pastor at our church, I am the associate pastor in charge of three ministries that include our care ministry. This means, more often than not, that I am walking with people who are hurting and broken. My activities include counseling people or couples, presiding over funerals, making hospital or home visits, and praying with people who are grieving great losses. At the time of this writing, I am ministering in this role to a congregation of around 5,000 souls. Needless to say, my days are long and exhausting.

One of the ways that I maintain my capacity to minister pursuant to my call is I get away once a month.[82] God has blessed me with a house that is two states (a five and a half hour drive) away from my primary home. This house is in a town where most people don't know me or what I do. It is my personal getaway and I feel the Lord's presence there more than anywhere else. I strongly urge you to find a place where you can go once a month to be renewed and refreshed in the Lord's presence. It doesn't have to be a place you own. There are many organizations and groups that operate retreat centers that specifically cater to pastors and, in many instances, their wives are also invited.[83]

God Days: I cannot take credit for this practice because I learned it from Pastor Matt Chandler of The Village Church in Dallas, Texas.[84] In case you don't know, The Village Church is one of the largest churches in the United States and Chandler, in addition to his lead pastor duties, is in much demand as a conference speaker and author. Like many pastors, those demands make it hard for him to spend time with the Lord.

Chandler teaches that pastors should consider spending what he calls a "God Day." He explains it as follows: schedule an entire day to be away from both your office and home. You cannot take any electronics with you – this includes computers, tablets, or any other devices that would allow you to get on email, Facebook, Twitter, or any other activity that would distract you. You can take your phone in case you need to call for help, but you must turn it off. All you need for the day is your Bible, something to write with, and a paper journal. The point of God Day is to spend time with the Lord praying, reading His Word devotionally, and listening to Him. Obviously, God Day is an activity that includes the spiritual disciplines of silence, solitude, prayer, and journaling. God Day is especially important if you find yourself struggling with finding time to engage in daily prayer and reading.

> ## NOTE TO CHURCH LEADERS
>
> You have an obligation to make sure that your pastor has an opportunity for devotional time, personal retreats, and God Days. Too often, I have seen churches (especially small ones) where pastors are expected to do everything and are overwhelmed by those duties to the point of burning out. Let's be clear — while the pastor is responsible for the congregation's care and spiritual feeding, there is no passage of Scripture that requires him to personally do all of it. Help your pastor by making sure people are trained who can handle non-preaching duties so that it is possible for him to have a devotional life that will greatly bless your church. I am very proud, for example, to belong to a church where our senior pastor enjoys a six-week sabbatical every summer. Make sure he gets time to get away to be refreshed and renewed spiritually, physically, and emotionally.

When all is said and done, maintaining your call depends on you keeping your soul. You cannot minister in God's power if you are not in constant fellowship and communication with the Father through His Son Jesus Christ and the Holy Spirit, who lives in you. The pastor's devotional life is critical to his ability and efficacy in shepherding the flock God has assigned to him. It is what Paul meant, when he wrote to Timothy, "rekindle the gift of God that is in you through the laying on of my hands".[85]

Maintaining the Communicated

"A call to pastor is a call to study." In Chapter 3 of this book, I shared that these words were spoken to me by a church elder who was encouraging me, in my call to pastoral ministry, by reminding me that a pastor must study God's Word to be effective. Paul gave Timothy this same advice in his second letter to him by writing, "Study to show yourself approved by God, a workman who need not be ashamed, rightly dividing the word of truth."[86] Hence, maintaining the communicated in our lives is about consistently studying God's Word.

Now if you are a young pastor or a seminary student preparing to become a pastor, this advice may seem to be a little too obvious to be useful. The truth is, however, that any experienced and mature pastor will tell you that the duties of caring for a growing congregation pose the constant danger of imposing on three areas of a pastor's life – his family time, his devotional time, and his study time. For this reason it is important that a pastor with a growing ministry be committed to the following steps with regards to his study time:

Calendar Management: It is critical that the pastor have a set time for studying God's Word, especially with sermon preparation in mind. Most pastors I know recommend the morning because it is when most of us are physically and mentally at our freshest. I am aware that there are many night owls out there who can study effectively at night. At age 56, however, I can tell you as a former night owl that this ability to study and retain information during the late hours of the day diminishes with age.

Pastors also differ in one other way regarding study time. Some pastors can study a few hours a day and can effectively learn their material in daily chunks. Other pastors need to commit longer periods of time to study because it takes them some time to ramp up and to disengage from study. The latter tend to set aside one specific day of the week for studying and will do so all day in preparation for their Sunday sermon. I prefer the one-day approach but it does have a drawback – if there is a death or tragedy in the congregation that you must attend to on that study day, you will have lost a large chunk of preparation time. The key here is for each pastor to know his own personal tendencies with regard to studying and to schedule his calendar accordingly.

A Suitable Study Environment: One way to assure that you are studying properly is to have an environment that is conducive to productive and meaningful study. I'm not talking about your local Starbucks or the library. The ideal location should be private, have a place for all of your books and materials, and should be inaccessible to distractions. Because I have adult children that have established their own homes, for example, I find that studying in my home office is the best way for me to avoid distractions and to study deeply and meaningfully in preparation for preaching. If you have young children, who can often create a great deal of noise and activity in your home, you may want to consider studying in your church office. Once again, know yourself and find what works best for you.

A Long-Term Plan: If God has called you to be a senior or lead pastor, you are the one ultimately responsible for all of the congregation's instruction. For this reason, it becomes important that you take time during the year to plan what you are going to teach your congregation. You must do this for two reasons. First, you need to make sure the congregation is getting balanced instruction in God's Word. Will the teaching on a specific Sunday be expositional or topical? If it's topical, will it be on a subject (like love) or a character (like Moses)? Will it be from the Old Testament or the New Testament? How will you tie each Sunday's sermon to the Gospel? How many Sundays will you dedicate to a guest preacher or another pastor on staff? Long term planning guarantees that your congregation is learning the entire Bible and not just the parts that you like, as well as receiving a well-balanced teaching to help them grow and mature as disciples.

The second reason you need to commit to long-term planning is that this exercise will help you to organize your study time. By knowing your subjects and themes in advance, you can decide issues like what materials are needed, what parts of the Bible will you study at specific times, and which subjects might require more concentration either because they are new to you or are not subjects you enjoy. I have to admit, for example, I am not as well-versed in the Minor Prophets as I am in the Pauline letters.

The bottom line is that long term planning can increase your effectiveness in studying God's Word by helping you to organize your time. I would be remiss, of course, if I didn't add that all of this planning should be done prayerfully and under the influence of the Holy Spirit.

Maintaining His Character

A pastor's prophetic call and his efforts in studying will all come to naught if he falls into sin because of his failure to maintain his character. I don't feel the need to add much more to this volume than what was covered earlier in Chapter 4, when I presented Paul's advice to Timothy with regards to the use of his tongue, conduct, purity, faith, and his love for others. The only advice I can add to all of this relates to one specific issue that I have seen pastors struggle with and that has been a huge contributing factor to their respective falls – the issue of accountability.

Pastors, especially senior or lead pastors, are some of the loneliest people I know. They often have no one to talk to because there is no one in their specific church community who can relate to the burden they carry. And, frankly, because there is such an expectation that the pastor be perfect in all that he does, he often doesn't feel like he can be vulnerable. Hence, in addition to a consistent devotional time with the Lord and studying His Word, the pastor must make sure to have an accountability partner or partners in his life that they can rely on for support.

There are two specific accountability partners I will discuss in this chapter and one more I will discuss in the next chapter on avoiding the force drain. The two sources of accountability I want to present here that can be of great comfort to a senior or lead pastor – the committed elder or the outside senior pastor. The committed elder can be an actual elder or trustee at your church or a mature man who is a key influencer in your congregation. This is an individual who demonstrates the ability to wear two hats – one as a church leader, but also one as a friendly mentor. One of the current elders of our church, for example, is in his 80's and was the executive pastor at another church many years ago. He is a deeply committed disciple of Jesus Christ, a deep well of wisdom, and is an generously patient listener. It is a great source of comfort to me that our church's senior pastor has the ear of such a wise, principled, and godly man, one that he can confide in whenever he needs to be vulnerable.

Another source of accountability for a pastor is other pastors. I'm very surprised to see that few pastors seek this option or make themselves available to connect with other pastors who often experience the same sense of loneliness, the same frustrations, and the same emotional challenges. I am aware that there are pastors who do this and are grateful to their colleagues for providing time to help them be vulnerable, real, and safe. But I believe those that connect with other pastors are in the minority. The Barna Group finds that this tendency to be disconnected is especially true of high-risk pastors – those with a higher tendency to burn-out or fall into sin.[87]

In the end, a pastor's ability to maintain his character depends on keeping a regular devotional time before the Lord, studying God's Word, but also keeping connected to a community of colleagues that will help him to process his emotions, express his frustrations, and prevent from falling into some of the pitfalls that lead to self-medication such as alcohol, affairs, and drugs.

Questions

1. How intentional are you in caring for yourself as a pastor? Does your calendar have time scheduled for you to care for yourself spiritually, emotionally, and physically?

2. Do you teach your congregation about the need to keep a Sabbath rest? If so, how well are you modeling this for them?

3. Do you feel that your elders, trustees, or congregation support your need for self-care?

Recommended Reading

1. Jim Loehr and Tony Schwartz. *The Power of Full Engagement*. New York, NY: Free Press Paperbacks, 2003.

2. Gordon MacDonald. *Ordering Your Private World*. Nashville, TN: Thomas Nelson, 2003.

7 AVOIDING THE FORCE DRAIN

If maintaining the three forces is about taking proactive steps to make sure that you are walking in your call, the communicated, and your character, avoiding the force drain is about guarding against conditions and situations that might diminish the working of the three forces in your life and ministry. What I call "force drains" fall into one of two categories – self-care and life calendar management.

Self-Care

Too many pastors give very little thought to the fact that maintaining your health is critical to your ability to minister to a congregation. Yet it is one of the issues that concerned the Apostle Paul in teaching Timothy on how to be a pastor. It appears young Timothy was having stomach troubles that were sufficiently severe so that Paul felt the need to advise him, "No longer drink only water, but use a little wine for the sake of your stomach and your frequent ailments."[88] The point here is that Paul was concerned for Timothy's health and, as a mature pastor, he understood the importance of maintaining good health as a prerequisite for an effective ministry.

There are six specific steps that a pastor can take to avoid the force drain in his life. These steps relate to:

Diet: American pastors have proven no less prone to being overweight than the rest of the U.S. population.[89] A good eating regimen is essential to maintaining the kind of health necessary to be an effective minister of the Gospel. The pastor's greatest enemies in this area of self-care are, first, the "on-the-run" meals (such as fast food or restaurant dining) when overwhelmed by a busy schedule and, second, culinary "love offerings" by those members of the congregation that like to indulge us with sweets and baked goods. If this is an issue for you, I want to suggest that keeping a food diary, which can be easily done today through smartphone apps, can help you to know and, if needed, change your eating habits.[90]

Physical Exercise: Having some kind of physical activity to help the body stay strong is very important. It can be something as simple as an upbeat walk or an activity you share with others, such as basketball or tennis. This is especially important because we can spend so much of our week sitting when we are studying, attending meetings, visiting with congregants. One recent trend that has been cited as being useful in helping individuals maintain fitness is working at standing desks. I have one colleague that still prefers to sit when he studies, but will stand when he is answering emails, working on slides, or reading the news on the Internet. In fact, he's gotten such great results that I recently adopted the same practice. The point here is to proactively combat undue weight gain and rapid physical deterioration by adopting some type of regular physical exercise activity. Needless to say, the development and use of an exercise routine should be done in consultation with your personal physician.

Medical Care: Speaking to your personal physician, regular check-ups, and medical visits are also important for the pastor's self-care, especially as we get on in age. It appears that one of the universal characteristics shared by men of all races and cultures is that we are all physician-adverse. Some of us are so bad about it that we must be dragged to the doctor's office by our wives, adult children, or good friends before we will get help whenever we are sick. I strongly advise finding a physician that you can bond with as a friend because it will help you to overcome any reluctance you may have to regular check-ups and visits. Your church should provide you with good health insurance so that economics are not a factor in whether you seek help or regular check-ups.

Emotional Care: I am a strong proponent of pastors having a therapist or counselor that they can go to for what I call "tune-ups." In Chapter 6, I discussed the importance of having an elder or another pastor to help maintain your character by providing accountability. I believe the tune-up is also important to maintaining your character in addition to helping you stay strong emotionally and spiritually.

The tune-up should be a monthly or quarterly appointment that you keep with a therapist or counselor, preferably one that does not belong to your congregation. I urge the latter because such a counselor can more easily maintain a higher level of objectivity and there's less of a chance that they'll inappropriately discuss any issues shared in a session with someone else in your congregation. These tune-ups are necessary for your emotional well-being because you regularly deal with people with intense and profound issues. Carrying someone else's divorce, suicide loss, financial failure, and cancer diagnosis can take a toll if you don't have somewhere safe where you can process the emotions tied to all of those life events. These visits should be covered by your health insurance also.

Hobbies: Finally, regarding this issue of self-care, the pastor should have some activity he enjoys that will build into him and keep him from being drained. Whether that activity is hiking, golf, chess, playing a musical instrument, or reading detective novels, it is a well-established fact that human beings need to have some type of activity that they enjoy, provides them with a deep sense of fulfillment, and can act as an outlet for their creativity. I play Afro-Latin percussion and often get to play for fun or with our church's worship team. If you don't have a hobby, you have one assignment resulting from the reading of this book – get a hobby!

The Habit of Delegation: In Chapter 4, I shared the fact that I often use *Acts 6* to teach on the importance of a pastor learning to delegate ministry tasks to qualified individuals. While I find this to be a common problem throughout African and Latin American churches, U.S. churches are not immune to this challenge. Too many pastors burn out because they are made to feel, or they themselves believe, that they must do it all. Remember in *Exodus 18*, when Moses' father-in-law saw him spending an entire day judging people's conflicts? Jethro said to Moses, "What you're doing is not good."[91] And what was his advice to Moses? "Delegate, delegate, delegate."

If you are a young pastor please begin to develop the habit of delegation. Identify people who are either highly gifted or who you can disciple to help you in your task of teaching and shepherding your flock. I am grateful for a senior pastor who trusts me and other clergy to preach for six weeks during the summer while he gets much needed rest and the opportunity to recalibrate. For older pastors, it might be harder for you to change if your congregation has gotten use to you doing everything. But the key to changing them is get your church leaders to help you change expectations and to slowly integrate the process of task delegation at your church. You'll be glad you did.

Calendar Management

In focusing on the pastor's need to study, I mentioned the importance of managing your calendar so that you can plan what you teach and when you will study in preparation for what you preach. I need you now to pull the lens back so that you can get a wider view – calendar management includes your taking steps to make space for everything in your life. I especially want to emphasize two important calendar management issues relating to your self-care as a pastor – your family and the need to say "no."

Family Time: Few things will devastate a family like a pastor's failure to guard his home life and allowing his pastoral duties to interfere with his home and family life. This is especially true when he fails to care for his marriage or in attending to his children. It is critically important for a pastor to remember that his first ministry is his home.

Regarding your wife, I would make two suggestions. First, schedule a regular "Date Night." There should be one night a week, or at least every month, when you can take her out and treat her to an evening of fun and pleasure. What you do depends on your budget and your access to babysitting, but in the end you must make time to focus on her so that you express your love and appreciation for who she is and all of her support. Second, and I especially offer this advice to young pastors or seminary students looking for their first job – do not allow your elders or congregation to highjack your wife!!!

One of the biggest crimes I have witnessed being perpetrated in the church is the practice by many congregations, especially smaller ones, of running a pastor's wife ragged with expected activities and duties that are unrewarded, with no financial compensation or remuneration offered whatsoever. This is particularly damaging to wives who are introverts and have not been equipped to run the ministries they are expected to lead. There is absolutely nothing in the Bible that requires a pastor's wife to be indentured to a congregation simply because they hired her husband. If you are a pastor, it is your duty to protect your wife by establishing boundaries on what she is willing to do for the church. The establishment of these boundaries should be done in consultation with your wife and need to be clearly communicated to your church leadership.

> ## NOTE TO CHURCH LEADERS
>
> Unless you sign a pastor's wife to a separate contract where she accepts the obligation to work for your church for compensation, you cannot legally obligate her to be the pastor's secretary, the head of the women's ministry, or the head of your children's program. Churches need to stop justifying this unholy practice of creating indentured servants of these women and using the Bible to justify it. If she volunteers, then praise the Lord. But if she chooses to concentrate on her home or some type of employment, please don't judge her. The expectation that hiring a pastor entitles you to his wife's services is simply unbiblical and inconsiderate.

The Need to Say "No": Younger pastors receive no training from their respective seminaries on developing this one skill – the ability to say "no." And yet, this is the most important skill in managing your time and your calendar. There are many things, including good ones, that you will have to say "no" to if you are to avoid the force drain in your life and ministry. As your ministry grows, you will be inundated with invitations and offers to all sorts of dinners, activities, and events. Your ability to say "no" depends on your having a clear picture in your mind of your priorities and of what comes first in your life and ministry. This was one of Stephen Covey's seven habits of highly effective people, better known as "Put First Things First."[92] This was the third habit and, in

Covey's mind, it was the culmination and physical manifestation of the first two habits – "Be Proactive" and "Begin with the End in Mind." How do these apply to you as a pastor and what does this all have to do with saying "no?"

It is critical for you to regularly consider your priorities as a husband, a father, and a pastor so that you can determine what to say "no" to as invitations and offers come along. I believe it is Timothy Keller who once said that we often say "yes" to good things at the expense of the best things. Ask the Lord to give you discernment when it comes to making choices on how to use your time. You are not being a bad pastor if you say "no" to something good because you are trying to honor your responsibilities as a husband and father.

The need to care for yourself is essential to your success as a pastor, especially if you are going to avoid those situations and conditions that will erode your call, the communicated, or your character. Attending to your well-being includes maintaining your devotional life, but also caring for yourself physically, mentally, and emotionally. Adopting healthy lifestyle habits can extend your ministry years by assuring that you are physically fit for the rigors of ministry.

Questions

1. How are you doing in defending against the "force drains" in your life?

2. Are you guilty of saying "yes" to good things at the expense of the best things?

Recommended Reading

1. John Ortberg. *Soul Keeping: Caring for the Most Important Part of You.* Grand Rapids, MI: Zondervan Publishing, 2014.

2. Stephen Covey. *Seven Habits of Highly Effective People.* New York, NY: Simon & Schuster, 1989.

8 CLOSING THOUGHTS

Paul's imperatives and commands to his sons in the faith are still relevant today to those of us called to the pastoral ministry. We are still required, as men chosen by God, to rely on our calling, to teach the communicated Word of God, and to maintain our character with due diligence and perseverance. The only question for us is how to channel these three forces, in our respective lives and ministries, in the current times that we live in.

Ministry in the 21st century has been complicated by the development of technology and, in particular, the growth and expansion of social media. I touched briefly, in Chapter 4, on how social media extends the reach of our words so that any misstatement or poorly considered comment can reach millions of people across the globe and change our lives drastically by bringing unwanted attention and judgment. Just ask Jen Hatmaker.

Hatmaker was for many years a popular Christian speaker and author on women's issues and ministry. She's written books that have made the New York Times best-seller list and even had, along with her husband, a very popular HGTV television show documenting the renovation of their home in Buda, Texas. In 2016, Hatmaker made two missteps that cost her many fans and book sales, but have even garnered her death threats. The first was posting on Twitter a direct challenge to any Christian leader who openly supported Donald Trump for president after the infamous "Access Hollywood" video tape was released.[93] Her misstep wasn't the fact that she raised concerns about Trump as a presidential candidate given the salacious and misogynistic nature of the comments made on the video, but it was the tenor and tone of the tweet – it was perceived as aggressive and disrespectful to leaders of the evangelical community.

Hatmaker's second misstep was an interview that she granted to Jonathan Merritt of the Religion News Service in which she announced her support for same-sex relationships. Hatmaker shares how people in her little hometown of Buda, just outside of Austin, began to pull her children to the side to tell them "terrible things about her and her husband."[94] In addition to the death threats, many people have mailed Hatmaker copies of her books that have been either cut-up or burned.

Regardless of your feelings about Hatmaker and her opinions about Trump or same-sex relationships, there is nothing in God's Word that can be used to justify death threats or even inappropriately speaking to her children. The more relevant point to this chapter, however, is that speaking openly in the age of social media has consequences that must be carefully considered.

Most pastors have received very little or no training in how to use social media platforms. As a result, they find themselves poorly equipped to either avoid the severe backlash resulting from a posted message containing a misstatement or on how to respond to overwhelming criticism when they have posted a Biblically correct statement or opinion that is extremely unpopular in our current cultural milieu. As a result, I strongly recommend that pastors get such training for themselves, their respective staffs, and their family members.[95] I repeat my warning to pastors from Chapter 4 – Paul's command to us from *Ephesians 4:29*, to speak with no unwholesome words, but only that which builds up, extends to our social media comments.

Another complication in the age of technology for the modern pastor is the issue of church growth and our nation's growing infatuation with experiencing life through its electronic devices. The church growth issue usually manifests itself in one of two questions – first, whether to stream services live on the Internet and, second, whether to accommodate church growth through the use of multi-site locations. While I do not currently possess either the expertise or experience necessary to make detailed comments on these issues, I do want to share two concerns as a fellow pastor who has sufficiently observed the interaction between people and technology to know that we need to be extremely careful.

Regarding the streaming of services, I am concerned that churches are undermining the sense of community that is supposed to result from discipleship with Jesus Christ. I know of too many people who are quite content to watch church on a device in the same way that they would enjoy watching movies on Netflix or a television program on Hulu. My concern here is twofold – first, that we may be leading people to engage in church as just another form of entertainment and, second, that we are helping them to violate God's Word in Hebrews, where it says "And let us watch out for one another to provoke love and good works, not neglecting to gather together, as some are in the habit of doing ..."[96] I'm not really sure how the streaming of services can build the type of community described in the Book of Acts.[97] Let me be clear – I am not against streaming services. What I am saying is that we need to be mindful of not leading disciples to disregard the Lord's command to assemble.

Multi-site churches have also become a popular way to either accommodate growing congregations or for churches to expand their respective reach in their community. In fact, our church is currently expanding to a nearby town by establishing our first multi-site location. That campus will have its own pastor and the church will offer a service that is live except for the sermon, which will be broadcast from our main campus. There are various churches that have successfully grown through this method, such as The Village Church in Dallas and The Crossing Church in the greater St. Louis area.[98] Despite this reported success, I share the concern various pastors have expressed about multi-site potentially creating a celebrity pastor culture, as well as its potential to undermine the pastor's role as a shepherd and role model.[99] Paul's instruction in the Pastoral Letters clearly anticipates a personal and intimate relationship between pastors and their respective members. I have not sufficiently studied the issue of multi-site locations to express an opinion on whether they are Biblical or effective. But I am concerned enough to say this – a pastor and church leadership should be careful to fully research and consider this method of church expansion before executing it. In particular, as churches seek to establish multi-site campuses, they must make sure there is a qualified and called pastor at each location who can walk closely with those congregants attending the campus he serves. I love a challenge that Jared Wilson gives to pastors because it applies to multi-site campus pastors as well. In writing about the need for pastors to be shepherds, he said, "Pastors, if you do not get to the end of your week without at least a little wool on your jacket, you might not be a shepherd."[100]

In the end, regardless of technology or the political state of our nation, those called to pastoral ministry are called to be shepherds. We are called to feed, tend to, and love God's people. Our ability to do so does not require us to be dependent on techniques, business concepts, or the latest fads. God has clearly called us, through the Apostle Paul's letters to his young charges, to be reliant on our call, His communicated Word, and the maintenance of our character. May you stand before the Lord on your final day of accounting and hear him say, "Well done, good and faithful servant."

ABOUT THE AUTHOR

Angel M. Cartagena is the Associate Pastor of Care and Adult Christian Education at Bridgeway Community Church in Columbia, Maryland. He is a native of Newark, New Jersey and a graduate of Yale University, Boston College Law School, and Northwestern Theological Seminary. A former attorney and government executive, Angel is the author of *The Success Continuum: Life's Path to Achievement* and has preached the Gospel of Jesus Christ around the United States and the world. He is currently living in Elkridge, Maryland with his wife, Wendy. They have three children – Kristin, Ruben, and Jasmin.

ENDNOTES

[1] Barna Group. (2017). *The State of Pastors*. Ventura, California: Dale Brown and Tod Brown, research sponsors.

[2] Ibid., 37.

[3] Ibid.

[4] Ibid., 47.

[5] This passage will be referred to throughout this book as our "key passage."

[6] See, *Acts 17:10-11*.

[7] *1 Timothy 1:18-19a*.

[8] *2 Timothy 1:6*.

[9] While Paul's letter to Titus contains no express statement regarding his being called to ministry, Titus' call can be implied from the fact that Paul instructed Titus to execute certain duties, such as the appointment of elders, that Timothy was also instructed to execute. See, *Titus 1:5*. In other words, Titus's call is implied by the fact that he is instructed to carry out the same duties as Timothy.

[10] John Henry Jowett, *The Preacher: His Life and His Work* (London: Hodder and Stoughton, 1912), 6.

[11] Charles H. Spurgeon, *Lectures to My Students* (Peabody, MA: Hendrickson Publishers, 2012), 25.

[12] Donald S. Whitney, "Pastor as Man of God" in *Portraits of a Pastor*. Edited by Jason K. Allen (Chicago, IL: Moody Publishers, 2017), 162-163.

[13] *Ephesians 4:12a*. Verse 11 is also important because it implies that the pastor's main function is to teach God's Word. This will be discussed in more detail in Chapter 3 below.

[14] *2 Timothy 1:6a* (Emphasis mine).

[15] *1 Corinthians 12:4-7.*

[16] *1 Timothy 1:18* (Emphasis mine).

[17] *1 Timothy 1:18* (NIV84) (Emphasis mine). HOLY BIBLE, NEW INTERNATIONAL VERSION®. Copyright © 1973, 1978, 1984 by the International Bible Society. Used by permission of Zondervan. All rights reserved.

[18] Howard F. Sugden and Warren W. Wiersbe, *When Pastors Wonder How* (Chicago: Moody Publishers, 1973), 9.

[19] Jowett at 14.

[20] While pastors are very much dependent on God's calling and the Holy Spirit to succeed in ministry, there are some things pastors can do in the flesh to increase the effectiveness in ministry. These will be discussed in chapters 6 and 7 of this book.

[21] Our practice is consistent with *Luke 16:10*, where Jesus is quoted as saying, "Whoever is faithful in very little is also faithful in much ..." The idea is for each of us in the church to demonstrate how much responsibility we can handle consistent with the gifts God has given us.

[22] See, *Acts 9:1-19.*

[23] *Matthew 7:28-29.*

[24] See, *Galatians 2:1-10.*

[25] *Galatians 2:2.*

[26] *Hebrews 13:17.*

[27] Bobby Jamieson, *Sound Doctrine: How a Church Grows in the Love and Holiness of God* (Wheaton, IL: Crossway, 2013), 17.

[28] *Titus 2:1.*

[29] *2 Timothy 2:15* (MEV).

[30] *Acts 6:2-4* (Emphasis mine).

[31] Jason G. Duesing, "Pastor as Missionary" in *Portraits of a Pastor*, Edited by Jason K. Allen (Chicago, IL: Moody Publishers, 2017), 137.

[32] See, *1 Timothy 5:1-16*.

[33] Jamieson at 20.

[34] *2 Timothy 1:5*.

[35] See, *Acts 16:1-3*. While we know Timothy's father was Greek, we do not know if he was an absent father or simply uninvolved in Timothy's life or upbringing. We can obviously imply from the Scriptures that Timothy's father allowed his mother and grandmother to take charge of Timothy's religious training.

[36] *2 Timothy 4:15*.

[37] *Luke 24:25-27*.

[38] *2 Timothy 3:16*.

[39] The ESV Study Bible®, Personal Size, ESV® Bible. Wheaton, IL: Crossway, 2008, p. 2342.

[40] Ibid.

[41] Kenneth S. Wuest, *Wuest's Word Studies from the Greek New Testament*, Vol. 2, (Grand Rapids, MI: Wm. B. Eerdmans Publishing Company, 1952), 150-151.

[42] The CSB, my primary Bible text for this book, translates "sound doctrine" as "sound teaching."

[43] John MacArthur, *Pastoral Ministry: How to Shepherd Biblically* (Nashville, TN: Thomas Nelson, 2005), 68.

[44] Whitney at 168.

[45] *1 Timothy 4:16*.

[46] See, Wayne Grudem, *Systematic Theology: An Introduction to Biblical Doctrine*, (Grand Rapids, MI: Zondervan, 1994), 788-806.

[47] Kenneth S. Wuest, *Wuest's Word Studies from the Greek New Testament*, Vol. 1, (Grand Rapids, MI: Wm. B. Eerdmans Publishing Company, 1952), 115.

[48] *James 3:6-8.*

[49] *1 Peter 3:15-16.*

[50] Emerson Eggerichs, *Before You Hit Send*, (Nashville, TN: W Publishing Group, 2017), xii-xiii.

[51] John F. Walvoord and Roy B. Zuck, General Editors, *The Bible Knowledge Commentary: New Testament*, (Colorado Springs, CO: David C. Cook, 1983), 741.

[52] See, *1 Timothy 5:17*, which says, "The elders who are good leaders are to be considered worthy of double honor, especially those who work hard at preaching and teaching."

[53] *1 Timothy 3:2-7.*

[54] Wuest, Vol. 2, 52-53.

[55] S. J. Robinson, *Opening Up 1 Timothy* (Leominster, MA: Day One Publications, 2004), 58.

[56] *Ephesians 5:1-2* (Emphasis mine).

[57] *1 Timothy 1:15.*

[58] Wuest, Vol. 2, 29.

[59] See, Dallas Willard, *The Spirit of the Disciplines: Understanding How God Changes Lives*, (New York, NY: HarperCollins Publishers, 1988), 156-191.

[60] Whitney at pp. 169-170.

[61] *1 Timothy 4:16.*

[62] *John 1:14, 17.*

[63] *Romans 2:1.*

[64] *Romans 14:10, 19.*

[65] *1 Timothy 1:5.*

[66] See, *John 21:15-19.*

[67] Jared C. Wilson, "Pastor as Shepherd" in *Portraits of a Pastor,* Edited by Jason K. Allen (Chicago, IL: Moody Publishers, 2017), 25.

[68] *2 Timothy 2:23-25a.*

[69] *Titus 3:9.*

[70] *1 Timothy 4:16.*

[71] *James 3:1.*

[72] *Hosea 4:4-6.*

[73] *Luke 8:17.*

[74] See, *Matthew 7:21-23.*

[75] *2 Timothy 4:3-4.*

[76] *2 Timothy 4:5.*

[77] Christopher Ash, *Zeal Without Burnout,* (Purcellville, VA: The Good Book Company, 2016), 24.

[78] Several of these books will be listed at the end of this chapter under "Recommended Reading."

[79] Prime and Begg, 82.

[80] Willard, 156-191. Willard lists seven spiritual disciplines of abstinence and eight spiritual disciplines of engagement that are helpful for connecting with the Lord. No one is expected to practice all 15 of them. Whenever I teach our congregation about these

disciplines, I emphasize that how many and which ones we practice usually depends on circumstances and the season of life that we find ourselves in.

[81] *Luke 5:16* (Emphasis mine).

[82] There are times when the demands of ministry and my schedule make my monthly retreat impossible. But when I don't take that time to get away, it negatively impacts my ability to serve.

[83] The American Association of Christian Counselors can provide good recommendations on various retreat centers that cater to pastors and their families.

[84] The video where Pastor Chandler teaches this concept can be found at https://youtu.be/tJprolu9S4A.

[85] *2 Timothy 1:6*.

[86] *2 Timothy 2:15* (MEV).

[87] *State of Pastors*, p. 42.

[88] *1 Timothy 5:23*.

[89] http://www.lifeway.com/pastors/2015/01/26/the-pastors-third-rail/.

[90] As an iPhone user I am very fond of the CalorieKing® app, which lets me track what I eat, how much exercise I get, and how much water I drink on a daily basis.

[91] *Exodus 18:17*.

[92] Stephen Covey, *The 7 Habits of Highly Effective People*, (New York, NY: Simon & Schuster, 2004), 154-191.

[93] Tiffany Stanley. *This Evangelical Leader Denounced Trump. Then the Death Threats Started.* (2017, December 17) Retrieved from Politico, https://www.politico.com/magazine/story/2017/12/17/is-jen-hatmaker-the-conscious-of-evangelical-christianity-216068.

[94] Ibid.

[95] Pastor Ron Carpenter of Redemption Church in Greenville, South Carolina, experienced the loss of many African-American church members when his wife posted a tweet attacking football player Colin Kaepernick for his decision to kneel during the national anthem to protest the many instances of police shootings of unarmed Africa-American victims.

[96] See, *Hebrews 10:24-25*.

[97] Luke described the original church in *Acts 2:42* by writing, "They devoted themselves to the apostles' teaching, to the fellowship, to the breaking of bread, and to prayer."

[98] The Village Church is currently executing a plan to turn each of its multi-site locations into independent congregations, using the multi-site method as a type of church planting technique.

[99] See, for example, John MacArthur's comments on Vimeo, which can be found at: https://vimeo.com/35703445.

[100] Wilson, 22-23.

Made in the USA
Columbia, SC
28 August 2018